■ MOSAIC I

A LISTENING/SPEAKING SKILLS BOOK

MOSAIC I

A LISTENING/SPEAKING SKILLS BOOK

With Learning Strategies and Language Functions
Second Edition

Jami Ferrer
University of Wisconsin, Madison
Goleta Union School District

Elizabeth Whalley
California Polytechnic State University, Pomona
San Francisco State University

with contributions by:

Marilyn Bernstein

Steven Carlson

Jill Wagner Schimpff

Steven Hollander

Steven Marx

McGRAW-HILL PUBLISHING COMPANY

New York   St. Louis   San Francisco   Auckland   Bogotá   Caracas
Hamburg   Lisbon   London   Madrid   Mexico   Milan   Montreal   New Delhi
Oklahoma City   Paris   San Juan   São Paulo   Singapore   Syndey   Tokyo   Toronto

This is an EBI book.

Mosaic I
A Listening/Speaking Skills Book

4 5 6 7 8 9 0   **DOH DOH**   9 4 3 2 1

ISBN 0-07-557556-6

This book was set in Aster by Dharma Press.
The editor was Mary Gill;
the text designer was Janet Bollow;
the cover designer was Cheryl Carrington;
the photo researchers were Stuart Kenter and Judy Mason;
the production supervisor was Renée Reeves.
R. R. Donnelley & Sons Company was printer and binder.

ACKNOWLEDGMENTS AND CREDITS

1 Hays, Monkmeyer. **2** Joseph Kovacs, Stock, Boston. **3** Donald C. Dietz, Stock, Boston. **13** © F. B. Grunzweig, Photo Researchers. **17** Ellis Herwig, Stock, Boston. **18** Elizabeth Crews, Stock, Boston. **22** Frank Siteman, EKM-Nepenthe. **26** Peter Vandermark, Stock, Boston. **27** © Jane Scherr, Jeroboam. **31** Positive Images, Stock, Boston. **32** © Ray Ellis, Photo Researchers. **35** © Erika Stone, Photo Researchers. **37** © Rollie McKenna, Photo Researchers. **39** Frank Siteman, Stock, Boston. **40** Copyright 1973 by the National Council on Family Relations, Fairview Community School Center, 1910 West County Road B, Suite 147, St. Paul, Minn. 55113. Reprinted by permission. **45** Robert Eckert, EKM-Nepenthe. **46** David Cherkis, EKM-Nepenthe. **51** © Science Photo Library, Photo Researchers. **55** NASA, Photo Researchers. **57** UPI/Bettmann Archive. **67** Courtesy of World Bank. **68** Hazel Hankin, Stock, Boston. **71** (left) © Carl Frank, Photo Researchers; (right) © Frederick Ayer, Photo Researchers. **72** (top) Courtesy of World Bank; (bottom left) Courtesy of Fireside Thrift Co., (bottom right) source: Merrill Lynch. **79** © Tim Davis, Photo Researchers. **80** Elizabeth Hamlin, Stock, Boston. **81** © Jan Halaska, Photo Researchers. **84** Owen Franken, Stock, Boston. **86** Peter Vandermark, Stock, Boston. **87** Suzanne Szasz, Photo Researchers. **92** Barbara Alper, Stock, Boston. **95** Courtesy of the Art Institute of Chicago. **99** *Zebras* by Victor Vasarely. Reproduced by permission of Fondation Vasarely, Musée de Gordes. **103** Jean-Claude Lejeune, Stock, Boston. **105** Owen Franken, Stock, Boston. **109** © Jon Wrice, Photo Researchers. **114** © C. Behnke, Animals, Animals. **115** UPI/Bettmann Archive. **119** Cary Wolinsky, Stock, Boston. **120** Ed Lettau, Photo Researchers. **129** © Michael C. T. Smith, Photo Researchers. **130** UPI/Bettmann Archive. **132, 133** Ira Kirschenbaum, Stock, Boston. **134** © Rex Weyler/Greenpeace. All rights reserved. **137** © Eileen Christelow, Jeroboam. **139** Owen Franken, Stock, Boston. **144** (top) © Omikron, Photo Researchers; (bottom) © Alexander Gardner, Photo Researchers. **145** UPI/Bettmann Archive. **148** Culver Pictures.

COVER

Robert Delaunay: *Landscape with Disk*, 1905
Oil on canvas, 21⅜ × 18″
Photographie Musée National d'Art Moderne, Centre Georges Pompidou, Paris

■ Contents

CHAPTER 4

Health

CHAPTER 5

Technology

CHAPTER 6

Money Matters

CHAPTER 7

Leisure Time

CHAPTER 8

Creativity

CHAPTER 9

Human Behavior

CHAPTER 10

Choices

CHAPTER 11

The Physical World

CHAPTER 12

Living Together on a Small Planet

■ Preface to the Second Edition

MOSAIC: THE PROGRAM

Mosaic consists of eight texts plus two instructor's manuals for in-college or college-bound nonnative English students. *Mosaic I* is for intermediate to high-intermediate students, while *Mosaic II* is for high-intermediate to low-advanced students. Within each level, I and II, the books are carefully coordinated by theme, vocabulary, grammar structure, and where possible, language functions. A chapter in one book corresponds to and reinforces material taught in the same chapter of the other three books at that level for a truly integrated, four-skills approach.

Each level, I and II, consists of four books plus an instructor's manual. In addition to *A Listening/Speaking Skills Book,* they include:

- *A Content-Based Grammar I, II:* Each grammar chapter relates to a specific theme, so the exercises focus on contexts and ideas. There is a wide variety of communicative, functional activities.
- *A Reading Skills Book I, II:* Selections in these books come from many sources, including newspapers, magazines, textbooks, and literature. The emphasis is on building reading and study skills; for example, skimming, scanning, determining the author's point of view, reading charts and graphs, guessing the meaning of new words from context, making inferences, outlining, and techniques for remembering what has been read.
- *A Content-Based Writing Book I, II:* These books provide students with short readings on the chapter themes and include many prewriting, revision, and vocabulary-building exercises. The books focus on the writing process, particularly on techniques for gathering ideas, such as "brainstorming" and "freewriting," and on using feedback to rewrite.
- *Instructor's Manual I, II:* These manuals provide instructions and guidelines for use of the books separately or in any combination to form a program. For each of the core books, there is a separate section with teaching tips and other suggestions. The instructor's manuals also include sample tests.

MOSAIC: A LISTENING/SPEAKING SKILLS BOOK

Mosaic I: A Listening/Speaking Skills Book is unique among listening/ speaking materials currently available. Most focus on either listening or speaking and teach either learning strategies or language functions. **This text teaches learning strategies *and* language functions,** while maintaining a strong focus on both listening *and* speaking. Interactive listening activities based on short but realistic academic lectures and sample conversations provide comprehension practice, while a variety of "real-world" speaking activities reinforce use in context of language functions.

Content of the sample lectures and conversations has been carefully chosen to appeal to the interests and needs of the students. The various learning strategies and language functions are thereby presented in a context of useful information. The interactive comprehension and production activities have also been carefully designed for maximum appeal to students. However, no two classes are alike, so activities are geared toward personalizing the learning process by allowing for a great deal of flexibility. The activities can generally be modified to reflect such things as local information, current events, names of students, and students' personal interests and experiences; teachers are encouraged to personalize the material whenever possible to keep student motivation high.

The text consists of twelve chapters. One learning strategy (Skill A) and one language function (Skill B) are presented in each chapter. The presentation of learning strategies and language functions throughout all twelve chapters is unique in its thoroughness and comprehensibility. Explanations include numerous pragmatic examples for application of both learning strategies and language functions. An abundance of idiomatic expressions are included. Also in each chapter is preparatory material in the form of an introductory paragraph, discussion items, a vocabulary exercise, and various photographs. Paralleling effective pre-reading strategies, these portions of the chapter help prepare the students for listening to the lecture by familiarizing them with vocabulary, getting them to recall what they already know about the topic, and stimulating interest and further questions.

This text is accompanied by a cassette program that contains the lectures and sample conversations for each of the chapters plus some explanatory comments. The conversations are printed in the student text; the lectures are not. Both appear in the key to the tape program, available from the publisher.

General Teaching Suggestions

1. Read through an entire chapter and listen to the taped material for that chapter before teaching any portion of it.
2. The book is intended to facilitate maximum student participation. During speaking activities respond to student requests for help, but as

much as possible allow students to interact without interruption unless there are misunderstandings or miscommunications. Keep notes, if you need to, and give feedback after students have completed an activity if you wish. You don't want students turning to you for a judgment after each sentence they utter.

3. To facilitate the various role-plays and other interactive activities, you will probably need to disinhibit yourself and the students to some degree. This is where you can really use the personal information you know about the students: what amuses them? what saddens them? what excites them? Plugging a few tidbits of personal information into an already relaxed and "safe" atmosphere can do wonders.

4. The exercises are designed to teach skills, not to test proficiency. But students will generally need to be reminded that it's all right to make errors; they are not expected to be competent at each task already, but, through the process of learning from errors, to *become* competent at the tasks.

5. This text provides more practice exercises and activities in each chapter than most teachers would be able to use in a week of class time. Thus, if you wish to do a chapter a week, you'll have to choose among the activities provided.

Chapter Organization and Specific Teaching Suggestions

Opening Photo   The opening photo can be used in combination with the chapter title for topic anticipation. Let students consider what could be included in the chapter given this particular photo. Or let the photo trigger whatever thoughts and discussion it might. About four to six minutes of discussion will be sufficient for most chapters, but you may want to spend a longer time if the discussion is particularly productive.

Introductory Paragraph   This paragraph focuses on the topic and provides a link between the chapter theme and content of the lecture. It can be assigned as homework, read silently or aloud in class, or perhaps read aloud by a student or the teacher with the students' books closed to provide additional listening comprehension practice.

Discussion   This section allows students to relate their own knowledge, background, and experience to the chapter topic. Rather than concentrating on what they don't know, they can focus on what they do know about the topic, thus building confidence to tackle the lecture material. There are *no right or wrong answers,* of course, and students should be encouraged to share whatever they can. In the course of the discussions, you will get to know the students better, and they will get to know each other better. Most questions are open ended, and you will want to plan how much time to allow for the questions. Fifteen minutes or so are suggested. You may wish to select certain questions and do only those. Sometimes you may wish to have students write out the answers for homework. This will allow you to find out how your most reluctant speakers would have answered the questions and give all students additional practice expressing themselves in English.

Vocabulary   The vocabulary items are fundamental for understanding the lecture and useful for the students in other contexts as well. The vocabulary exercise may be assigned and done in class or as homework. Sometimes you may want students to work on these in groups to provide additional speaking practice. When pressed for time you can quickly read the correct answers to students and discuss only particular items that were problematic. Answers are in the instructor's manual.

Skill A   The study skills in this section are essential for academic success. An explanatory presentation is provided for each skill: the students should read this at home or in class before you discuss the skill with them. You might want to put key points on the board during the discussion.

Listen In, Skill A   Students listen to the lecture and do the accompanying listening exercise. You may want to follow the procedure described in the text for listening to the lecture, or you may choose your own procedure. For example, after the first listening you may have students listen again and write down any words they don't understand or take notes. Or you may want to stop the tape periodically and have students paraphrase what they have heard. Then do the exercise provided in the text. The answers are provided in the instructor's manual.

Speak Out, Skill A   The *Speak Out* activities allow students to get further practice of a skill in context. The focus is on speaking, but the exercise also involves listening to fellow students. Both whole-class and small-group activities are provided, and you may wish to vary the suggested group size. Sometimes it is advisable to put all the stronger students in one group so that they cannot dominate the weaker students. At other times it is advisable to have the stronger students dispersed among the class. It is inadvisable to allow students to form their own groups if they don't vary the groupings. Periodically changing group make-up promotes strong class rapport as well as provides a greater variety of voices and speaking styles for listening practice. The *Speak Out* activities vary in length from ten minutes to a whole class period.

Skill B   A language function is explained to the students and then is demonstrated through short conversations presented in the text and on tape. Here students learn appropriate and inappropriate use of idioms, intonation, and body language associated with the function. The conversation can be presented in several ways:

1. Students read along as they listen.
2. Students listen with books closed.
3. Students listen and repeat (when dialogues are short or you can stop the tape to allow for this).

4. Students listen and pantomime facial expressions and gestures they think the speakers would use.
5. The dialogues are also quite suitable to be modified as cloze passages with the students filling in key words as they listen.

Listen In, Skill B This section gives the students the opportunity to listen for uses (or misuses) of the language function in the lecture and (in some chapters) in the conversations. Answers to the exercise and provided in the instructor's manual.

Speak Out, Skill B These activities provide natural language contexts in which to practice the language function. They are designed to maximize student interaction and verbal output. The teacher should provide feedback that does not inhibit this process as the students play the various games, participate in role-plays, or team up for debates. The amount of time you spend can vary from a brief period to a whole class hour.

ACKNOWLEDGMENTS

Both people and places have contributed to this book. First, we wish to acknowledge the people whose expertise and imagination provided not only inspiration but manuscript pages as well: Marilyn Bernstein, Steven Carlson, Jill Wagner Schimpff, Steven Hollander, and Steven Marx. We extend our gratitude to those who provided invaluable suggestions as we faced deadlines: Bonnie Anthony and her students; Tom and Jean Atherton; Steve Aron; Connie Bendel; Leon Bloomfield; Lauri Carlson; Mary Dunn; Ann Feldman; Mark Ferrer; Jane Gray; Chris Hepburn; Alicia, Evie, and Sally Klein; David Marimont; Alan McCornick; John and Susan Nelson; Michael Smith; Billie Lynn and Mickey Strauss; Ann Stromberg; Pat Sutton; Patty Werner; and Gertrude Whalley.

We also wish to thank the following reviewers whose comments, both favorable and critical, were of great value in the development of this text: Tiby Appelstein, Newbury Junior College; Lida Baker, University of California at Los Angeles: Ellen Broselow, State University of New York, Stony Brook; Van Caliandro, Bronx Community College, City University of New York; Ellen Garshick, Georgetown University; Barbara Gray, Polytechnic Institute of New York; Anne Hagiwara, Eastern Michigan University; Nancy Herzfeld-Pipkin, San Diego State University; Patricia Johnson, University of Wisconsin, Green Bay; Gail Kellersberger, University of Houston; Nancy Lay, City College, City University of New York; Tamara Lucas, San Francisco State University and Stanford University; Roy Ludtke, Arizona State University; Debra Mathews, University of Akron; Pamela McPartland, Hunter College, City University of New York; Paul Most, University of California at Los Angeles; Maryanne O'Brien, University of Houston; Helen Polensek, Oregon State University; Amy Sonka; Stephanie Vandrick, University of San Francisco. Special thanks to Sandra McKay for her review of the entire manuscript.

We heartily acknowledge libraries, restaurants, parks, pools, and people's homes that were so graciously opened to us as havens during long hours of work and give special thanks to librarian Diane Stoll for tirelessly searching for material with a minimum of clues, to the Cal Poly Faculty Development Program, to Thomas and Judith Wasow for use of their lovely home, and to John and Mary Gill for sacrificing their privacy for the sake of the project.

Finally, we wish to express our deepest appreciation to Deana Fernández for her undaunted word processing and valuable editorial suggestions, to Eirik Børve who included us in this ground-breaking project, and to Janet Bollow Associates for their excellent work on the design of the text. Most of all, we are ever grateful to Mary McVey Gill for her monumental efforts in pulling such a project together, her most excellent editorial work, and her friendship.

J. F.
E. W.

MOSAIC I

A LISTENING/SPEAKING SKILLS BOOK

CHAPTER 1
NEW CHALLENGES

Part of the enormous challenge of our complex world is to learn to understand other people and to make ourselves understood. Sometimes we do this successfully and sometimes not. It is certainly a challenge to communicate with someone who speaks a foreign language. But it can also be challenging to communicate with someone who speaks our native language but has a very different perspective on the world. The lecture in this chapter is titled "Learning to Speak Someone Else's Language." It might be the first lecture in a course on communication theory.

Lecture: Learning to Speak Someone Else's Language

Skill A: Listening to Make Predictions

Skill B: Offering and Requesting Clarification

PART ONE

DISCUSSION

Get into groups of three to discuss the following.

1. Have you ever had an experience like the following one? You are vacationing or traveling in a place where you do not know anyone. No one knows who you are, either. You find yourself

behaving differently than "normal." Try to recall an experience like this in detail. Share your memories with two classmates. Include answers to these questions:

a. *Where* were you?
b. *What* did you do?
c. *Why* did you do what you did?
d. Is it sometimes easier to open up to people who don't know you? Why is this so?

2. Someone once said that getting to know someone is like peeling an onion; we have layers that are slowly and carefully peeled off. Do you agree with this idea? Why or why not?

3. Has your study of English changed you in any way? If so, how? For example, has it made you more outgoing? Has it made you more or less critical of how people speak your native language? Has it made you more or less tolerant of other cultures? Has it changed your understanding or opinion of human nature?

VOCABULARY

The italicized words in the following sentences are used in the lecture in this chapter. Some of these words express concepts directly related to the topic. Others are used when the lecturer wants to give an example of something. Choose the best definition for the italicized word or words in each sentence and put the appropriate letter in the space provided.

1. _____ As your lecturer prepared this lecture for you, he looked at the *collage* made of paper, wood, paint, leaves, and glue hanging on the wall of his office.

2. _____ He is *hypoglycemic;* he can't eat much sugar or he gets sick.

3. _____ As a professor of *linguistics,* he is interested in the study
_____ of language *acquisition.*

4. _____ According to your instructor, because language is very complex and not at all straightforward, it presents us with many *paradoxes.*

5. _____ For many years, researchers thought we learned lan-
_____ guage through *imitation* of others and *association* of words.

6. _____ However, Noam Chomsky, a famous linguist, suggested that the ability to learn a language is *innate.*

3

7. _____ Learning to speak someone else's language can *fundamentally* change us.

8. _____ As we learn to speak someone else's language, we may *transform* our concepts about the world.

    a. connection (in the mind)
    b. to change the fundamental nature of something
    c. an artistic composition of materials and objects pasted over a surface
    d. having to do with the foundation; basically
    e. the science of language; the study of the nature and structure of human speech
    f. a physical condition resulting from an abnormally low level of sugar in the blood
    g. present at birth; inborn
    h. the act of acquiring or obtaining; development
    i. statement or situation that presents opposing views as true at the same time
    j. modeling one's behavior on the behavior or actions of another

PART TWO

SKILL A: LISTENING TO MAKE PREDICTIONS

Part of the nature of life is that we can never be absolutely sure what will happen next. Surprises can be nice in everyday life, but if they occur frequently when we listen to a lecture, the lecture may seem difficult to understand. In order not to be surprised too often, it is useful to stay one step ahead of the instructor and anticipate what the instructor will say next in the lecture.

In order to do this, first try to predict what the lecturer will cover. As you think about the title of the lecture, think about what you already know about the topic. Think too about what parts a lecture with this title might have. This will give you more ideas about what to expect in the lecture, and most likely it will also bring to mind a variety of questions. If you are curious about the topic, you will be more interested in the lecture.

Second, as you listen to the lecture, you can make more specific predictions about what the lecturer will say. As the lecturer progresses, you have more and more information to use to make your predictions. The pattern goes like this:

- The lecturer makes a statement.
- You predict what he or she will say next.
- You judge quickly whether you were right or wrong.
- If you were right, fine.
- If not, you must consider what was actually said and base your predictions on that.

There's a bonus that comes with the skill of listening to make predictions. As you focus on the lecture in this way, you become more involved. When you are really involved in listening, you are less likely to be distracted by thoughts of things such as lunch, your soccer game, or the date you had on Saturday night.

Listen In

Your instructor will write the title of the lecture on the blackboard. Use the title to predict what might be included in the lecture. Your instructor will write the class's predictions on the board exactly as they are given.

Now listen to segments of the lecture one at a time. This will give you the opportunity to understand what has been said already and to predict what will come next. This is exactly what you should do in an actual classroom lecture. However, here you will have more time to master this active listening skill. Your instructor will write your predictions on the board. The quotes from the lecture indicate where you should stop the tape.

Stop 1 ". . . they are still challenging to me now that I am a professor of linguistics, teaching courses on communication theory."
Predict what questions the lecturer will ask.

Stop 2 ". . . and can we ever really learn to speak someone else's language?"
Did you predict some of the questions the lecturer asked? What do you think he will say in the next few minutes?

Stop 3 "But learning to speak languages seems to be a very mysterious process."
Your lecturer has been discussing some of the problems with communication. In the last segment you listened to, he started to make a transition from the topic of communication breakdown to the topic of successful communication. He suggested that learning to speak languages seems to be a very mysterious process. What do you think he will discuss next?

Stop 4 "Chomsky's theories suggest something about the structure, or grammar, of language, but not very much about how it is used."

You recorded some predictions on the board before this section. Did you make some correct predictions? What do you suppose the lecturer will talk about next? Continue recording your responses on the board.

Stop 5 ". . . The rules of our native language . . . can actually determine whatever meaning we find in the world."

According to your lecturer, we can view the world from another perspective if we can learn to speak someone else's language. What consequences do you think this might have? Write down what you think will come next.

Listen to the rest of the lecture and, if you wish, listen to the entire lecture again. Then, as a class, analyze your predictions.

1. Were you able to make accurate predictions?
2. How might you use such a technique during a real lecture?

Speak Out

Exercise 1 For each of the following scenarios, predict what you think will occur. Don't tell anyone your predictions; just write what you think will happen in the spaces provided after each scenario. Include in your predictions whether the characters in the scenario will communicate well ("speak each other's language") or whether they will have a basic misunderstanding due to their different per-

spectives. Several possibilities are given as examples for the first scenario.

1. *Character 1:* A short gentleman, about sixty-five years old.
   Character 2: A tall lady, about seventy-five years old.
   Scenario: The lady and gentleman meet in front of the only empty seat on a crowded New York City subway. If the man sits down, he is being impolite. If he stands up, he may fall because he is too short to reach the strap.

   Your prediction:

   Example: *The woman convinces the man to sit down. They start talking. Both of them miss their stops. They communicate well and agree to get off the subway at the next stop and have coffee together.*

   Example: *The man gives the seat to the woman. When the subway starts suddenly, he falls into her lap. They communicate well and they laugh and say the transit authority should have more subways during rush hour.*

   Example: *The man and woman see the seat at the same moment. They communicate poorly and, while they are arguing, someone else comes along and sits in it.*

2. *Character 1:* An eighteen-year-old rock musician who is kind, gentle, and loves his mother. His father died when he was a small boy.
   Character 2: A loving but very conservative mother.
   Scenario: The rock musician wants to have his ear(s) pierced, but only wants to do it with his mother's permission. The mother and son are sitting in the living room discussing the pros and cons of ear piercing.

   Your prediction: _____

   _____

   _____

   _____

3. *Character 1:* A shy young man, twenty-five years old.
   Character 2: A liberated young woman, twenty-three years old.
   Scenario: The young man and young woman met five and a

half weeks ago. She would like to marry him. He would like to marry her. They're finishing a romantic dinner at a very nice restaurant. Both the young man and the young woman are trying to figure out a way to bring up the topic of marriage.

Your prediction: _____

_____

_____

_____

4. *Character 1:* A young man named Harry, twenty-two years old, with two tickets to a soccer match.
Character 2: A young man named Bob, twenty-two years old. Bob has a passion for soccer and a chemistry midterm exam tomorrow.
Scenario: Bob and Harry are in the Student Union at 3:00 P.M. They are drinking coffee. Harry is trying to convince Bob to go to the soccer match.

Your prediction: _____

_____

_____

_____

5. *Character 1:* A student.
Character 2: A grocery store clerk, a student and friend of Character 1.
Scenario: The first student is at the checkout stand of the store with $83 worth of soft drinks, pretzels, potato chips, cheese, crackers, beer, and wine for a party. He finds he has only $64 cash with him and no checks. The clerk at the store is a close personal friend of Character 1 but has not yet been invited to the party.

Your prediction: _____

_____

_____

6. *Character 1:* A freshman at Needles College named Randy who is not athletic at all and always makes jokes about exercising.
Character 2: A freshman at Red River College named Sandy who is very athletic and jogs every day.
Scenario: Before the two young women, Randy and Sandy, who are very good friends, went off to college in September, Randy said: "I bet I'll lose ten pounds by Thanksgiving and

you won't." Each young woman placed a secret note that said "If I lose ten pounds and you don't, you have to _____" inside an envelope. Now it is Thanksgiving vacation. First the young women open the envelopes and read the notes. Then they each get on the scale.

Your prediction (be sure to include what each young woman wrote in her secret note): _____

_____

_____

_____

7. *Character 1:* A widowed father living in Chicago.
   Character 2: His son, age fifteen.
   Scenario: The father has been offered a good position with higher pay in Toronto and wants to move. But his son does not want to leave Chicago, his high school, and all his friends. They are discussing this at the breakfast table.

   Your prediction: _____

   _____

   _____

8. *Character 1:* An "A" student who just got a failing grade for the first time on a midterm exam.
   Character 2: A professor, about forty years old, who is tough but usually fair.
   Scenario: It is the professor's office hour, and the student is explaining why he or she failed the exam. The student tells the professor about a personal problem and asks to take the exam again.

   Your prediction: _____

   _____

   _____

9. *Character 1:* The father of a three-day-old baby.
   Character 2: The mother of the baby.
   Scenario: The law in the place where the characters live requires that parents choose a name for their baby after three days. The mother wants to name the baby Sunshine; the father hates that name and wants to name the baby Hester, after his mother.

Your prediction: _____

_____

_____

_____

10. *Character 1:* Josephine, an art student who just moved into a new apartment.
Character 2: Rob, a business major and a friend of Josephine's.
Scenario: Josephine is in her new apartment, hanging some pictures on the wall. The doorbell rings and Rob walks in with a gift, a picture for her apartment. Josephine thinks it is the ugliest picture she has ever seen.

Your prediction: _____

_____

_____

_____

Exercise 2   Choose a partner for the next part of this activity. Then choose one of the previous scenarios for you and your partner to act out. It doesn't matter which one you choose or if more than one pair of students chooses the same scenario.

Plan your role-play with your partner. You may use the prediction that you wrote for the scenario you and your partner chose to do, the one your partner suggested, or a third, quite different, prediction. When you and your partner are ready, probably after ten to twelve minutes, present your role-play of what happens next between the people in your scenario to the rest of the class.

After each pair of students presents a role-play, share the predictions you all wrote about that scenario. Did anyone in the class predict what happened during the role-play? Were any predictions similar or were they all quite different? If there were similarities, why do you think they occurred? Do you think your individual perspectives (your private languages) account for the variety of predictions? Discuss why or why not. Did you feel that someone else's prediction was more likely to occur than yours? Why or why not?

SKILL B: OFFERING AND REQUESTING CLARIFICATION

Most often when we give information to people, we want them to understand it and remember it. An instructor speaking about linguistics, a policeman giving directions to the post office, a friend giving a shopping list for a party, and an employee listing recent company sales data all want listeners to understand and remember what they said.

All of us, however, have noticed that sometimes people don't seem to be following what we are saying. These listeners might look puzzled, with their eyebrows pulled together. Or they might appear tense or nervous as they keep trying to understand. Listeners who are not following what we are saying may simply not be paying attention. In this case, we may see a dreamy look in their eyes.

One way to make sure that people will understand and probably remember what we are saying is to offer clarification when it is needed. That is, we can either repeat the information exactly or say it again in another way. To find out if clarification is needed, we can check with the following expressions:

Are you following me?
Are you with me?
Did you get that?
Do you understand so far?   Appropriate for
Does that make sense to you?   most situations
Is that clear?
Okay, so far?

Did you catch that?   Not appropriate for
Got it?   formal situations

When you use these expressions to check whether people need clarification or not, listeners are usually appreciative. But be careful with your tone of voice. Some of the expressions can easily sound like reprimands, and you'll sound as if you were angry because they weren't listening. Unless you are speaking to a very naughty child, this is extremely inappropriate and very rude.

Listen to the following speakers. Each of them uses the same expression to try to find out whether the listener is following what has been said. But the effects are very different.

Conversation 1

Mrs. Garcia: To figure out the daily costs you'll have to add up all the numbers in Column A, divide by 30, and then multiply by the number of days you'll be there. Is that clear?

In this case, the speaker is polite and helpful. The speaker wants only to clarify the information if necessary. Now listen to this.

Conversation 2

Mrs. Smith: No, you can't watch t.v. First you have to clean up your room, write a thank-you note to your grandmother for your birthday present, put your bicycle away, take your model airplane project off the kitchen table, put your library books in the car so we can return them tomorrow, finish your homework, and take out the garbage. Is that clear!

Clearly, this is a reprimand. The mother is angry and does not really want to repeat this information. Most likely this is because she's already said this many times before.

Now you have some idea how to make sure the listener is understanding when you are the speaker. When you are the listener, however, you cannot be certain that the speaker will offer clarification to you in this way. Therefore, when you do not understand what someone is saying, don't wait for them to ask you if you understand or not. In this case, you should request information immediately. This may mean that you will have to interrupt the speaker. To do this politely, use the following expressions:

One of these:	*Followed by one of these:*
Could/Can/May I interrupt?	Could you/Would you mind repeating that?
	Could/Would you repeat that please?
Excuse me.	Could/Would you say that again please?
Pardon me.	I didn't get the last part (word, etc.).
I beg your pardon.	What was that again?
I'm sorry.	

In informal situations, the following expressions are commonly used to request clarification:

Huh?

I didn't get the last part (word, etc.).

I didn't catch that.

What?

What did you say?

You lost me.

Listen In

Listen to the lecture once again. Did you notice that the lecturer uses several of the expressions for offering clarification? Most speakers will use some of these expressions more than once and other expressions not at all. Using the same expressions repeatedly is part of a lecturer's style. Being familiar with a lecturer's style can help you understand the content more easily.

Listen to the lecture again. As you listen, notice which expressions the lecturer uses to offer clarification. Each time the lecturer uses a particular expression, make a mark next to it in the "Skill

Every day many cultures mingle in Central Park, New York City.

B" section. Which ones does he use frequently? (Or which are his favorites?) Which ones doesn't he use? Did you need clarification when the lecturer offered it? Were there times when you needed clarification and the lecturer did not offer it?

Listen to the lecture again. And this time, stop the tape and request clarification when you need it. If you are listening to the lecture by yourself, stop the tape whenever you do not understand something. Use one of the expressions listed in "Skill B" to request clarification. Then rewind the tape a little and listen to that section of the lecture again. If you are listening to the lecture with your classmates during class, raise your hand when you do not understand something. Your instructor will stop the tape so that you may request clarification, either from your instructor or from your classmates. Try not to use the same expression each time you request clarification; instead, practice using a variety of expressions for this purpose. Be ready to help your classmates, if you can, when they request clarification.

Speak Out

Choose a partner for this activity. Take turns presenting the following challenging problems to each other. Some of them are riddles and others might be called "brain teasers." As you do them, you'll understand why. (The answers are on page 150.) Proceed with the activity in this way:

- *Presenter:* Read the problem to your partner as quickly as you can. Do not pause at all, not even for a breath.

■ *Listener:* Keep your book closed. Do not read along with your partner. If you do not understand something and need clarification, tell your partner this. Use one of the expressions in the "Skill B" section.

■ *Presenter:* Read the problem again. This time, slow down a little and frequently use expressions to check if your partner needs clarification.

■ *Listener:* Tell your partner if you still need clarification.

■ *Presenter:* Slow down even more if necessary.

■ *Listener:* Try to solve the problem.

When you have done all the problems with your partner, compare your answers with those of your classmates.

Problems

1×2×3×4 ×{×6 ×7 × ---- ×0 =0

1. How much is 1 times 2 times 3 times 4 times 5 times 6 times 7 times 8 times 9 times 0?

2. Write down this eight-digit number: 12,345,679. <u>Multiply</u> this number by any *one* of these eight numbers. Now multiply by 9. What did you get? Try it again, but this time multiply by another of the eight digits before you multiply by 9. What did you get this time? *12345679 ×1 ×9= 111,111,111*

12345679 ×2 ×9
= 222,222,222

3. Mary lives on the twelfth floor of her apartment building. When she wants to go to her apartment, she gets into the elevator in the lobby and pushes the button for the sixth floor. When the elevator arrives at the sixth floor, she gets off and walks up the stairs to the twelfth floor. Mary prefers to ride the elevator, so why does she get off and walk up the stairs?

she is

4. Farmer Higg owns three pink pigs, four brown pigs, and one black pig. How many of Higg's pigs can say that they are the same color as another pig on Higg's farm? *Pig cant talk*

5. What is it that occurs once in a minute, twice in a moment, yet not at all in a week?

6. Think of a number from 1 to 20. Add 1 to this number. Multiply by 2. Add 3. Multiply by 2. Subtract 10. Tell me the answer and I'll tell you the number you started with.

2+1 ×(2) +3× (2) -10
= 8

7. A man wants to cross a river. He has a lion, a sheep, and a bale of hay that he must take with him. He has a boat, but it will carry only him and one other thing. So the trouble is, if he leaves the lion alone with the sheep, the lion might eat the sheep. If he leaves the sheep alone with the hay, the sheep might eat the hay. How does he get himself, the lion, the sheep, and the hay to the other side of the river?

8. The governor of Goleta wants to give a small dinner party. He invites his father's brother-in-law, his brother's father-in-law, his father-in-law's brother, and his brother-in-law's father. How many people does he invite?

(6)   5
     +1   Add, plus
     =6   = equals
     ×2   ×   Multiply, times
     =12
     +3
     15
     ×2
     30
     −10
     20 ⟶ Subract

CHAPTER 2
ACADEMIC LIFE

One of the major ways we learn is by listening. Because listening is so important to the learning process, it is a skill that is taught in special study-skills courses along with note taking, reading, vocabulary building, and taking exams. Study-skills courses are offered at most colleges. Students who want to improve the skills that are necessary for a successful academic life take these courses. Sometimes freshmen are required to take them. The lecture in this chapter is for a course in study skills.

Lecture: Learning to Listen/Listening to Learn
Skill A: Listening for the Main Ideas
Skill B: Asking for Confirmation

PART ONE

DISCUSSION

As a class, discuss the following.

1. How much time do you spend sleeping? Speaking? Listening? Reading? Writing? Awake but not communicating? On the following scale, indicate how much of each day you think you spend in these activities by placing a check under the appropriate percentage.

Sometimes we listen, sometimes we don't.

	0%	25%	50%	75%	100%

Sleeping: _____

Speaking: _____

Listening: _____

Reading: _____

Writing: _____

Awake but
not commu-
nicating: _____

Compare your scale with your classmates' scales. Are the scales similar or do they vary quite a bit? Discuss the similarities and differences. Share the reasons you marked particular percentages on your scale. Were they similar to your classmates' reasons, or different?

2. How fast do you think people speak? Seventy-five words per minute? One hundred twenty-five words per minute? Two hundred? Two hundred seventy-five? Your teacher will speak to you for one minute about his or her past academic life (elementary, secondary and college-level educational experiences). In the space provided, make a mark (卌 |||) for each word that is spoken. Then, in groups of three or four, take turns speaking for about one minute about your past academic lives. In the spaces provided, make a mark for each word your classmates speak.

Words Spoken in One Minute

Teacher: _____

_____

Student A: _____

_____

Student B: _____

_____

Student C: _____

_____

Compare the results in your group with the results of the other groups in your class. What is the average rate of words spoken in one minute? Do you think this is a lot of words to understand in one minute or not very many words? Do you think you speak faster in your native language? Do you think native English speakers talk too quickly for you to understand them?

3. Here's some good news! People can understand more words per minute than people generally speak per minute. At what rate do you think people can understand the spoken language? Two hundred words per minute? Three hundred words per minute? Four hundred? Four hundred fifty? Mark down your guess. The lecture in this chapter will reveal the answer as well as some other interesting things about listening skills and how they can be improved.

VOCABULARY

Exercise 1   Fill in the blanks with the correct forms of the following words.

counterexample	*an example that demonstrates an opposite view*
gist	*main idea*
to stick with	*to keep working on, stay with*
uncomplicated	*simple, easy to understand*
upcoming	*going to happen in the near future*

1. The thing I like about Professor Crawford's lectures is that they are very straightforward and completely

   _____.

2. I knew the lecturer was wrong because I could easily think

   of a _____.

3. What I like about Rose-Marie is that she always

   _____ her projects and never gives up until they are finished.

4. "I can always get the _____ of what Professor McClellum says, but because of his Scottish accent, I never understand every word," said Julian.

5. I'm really nervous about my _____ exam.

Exercise 2   Share your answers to the following questions with your classmates.

1. "Women are just no good at mathematics. I've never met a woman in my country who was a math major." From your own experience, what is a good counterexample to the previous statement?

2. Think of the last lecture or film that you attended, either here or in your native country. Briefly, what was the gist of it?

3. Do you think there is a difference between being a "quitter" and knowing when (the right time) to quit? Do you always stick with everything you start no matter what the circumstances are? Why or why not?

4. What kind of homework is the most complicated for you? What kind is the most uncomplicated? Why?

5. What are one or two upcoming events in your life?

PART TWO

SKILL A: LISTENING FOR THE MAIN IDEAS

Discovering the main ideas in a lecture is an extremely important skill to develop. The main ideas are what the lecture is about. Usually there is an overall main idea. This is the one idea that you can state briefly when a classmate asks you, "What was the lecture about?" In most cases, there are several other main ideas in addition to the overall one. The main ideas are the messages that lecturers most want you to remember, to take away from the lecture hall with you. These are the ideas they hope will stick with you for a long time.

Along with the main ideas, lecturers usually present examples and details that may include illustrations and data. Basically, lecturers present main ideas and supporting information in two ways: the deductive and inductive methods. The following diagram illustrates the differences between these methods.

Deductive	**Inductive**
Main Idea	Examples or Details
Examples or Details	Main Idea
Main Idea	Examples or Details
Examples or Details	Main Idea
Main Idea	Examples or Details
Examples or Details	Main Idea

If a lecturer starts out with the main idea, he or she is using the deductive method. If the lecturer starts out with examples or details, the inductive method is being used. You do not need to learn the names of these methods. However, it is helpful for you to recognize the pattern of presentation of the main ideas, examples, and details.

Sometimes lecturers mix these two ways of presenting information, which can be confusing. If your instructor does this, you

should rewrite your notes as soon as possible after class and ask questions about any points that are confusing to you.

Listen In

The following exercise will help you listen for the main ideas in the lecture. The details are on the left-hand side of the page. Read them first. Then listen to the lecture. As you listen, fill in the main ideas on the right-hand side of the page. The first one has been done for you. You will probably want to listen to the lecture more than once.

Details

A. We can reread, but we cannot relisten to a message.

B. We can control the speed when we read, but we can't when we listen.

C. When we listen we must understand immediately, since we can't use a dictionary easily.

A. Think ahead.

B. Evaluate what the speaker says.

C. Review what has been said.

Main Idea

I. _Reading and listening are different in three ways._

II. _____

A. People are less likely to daydream when taking notes.

B. Notes make it easier to review.

C. Notes can remind you of information you have forgotten.

III. _____

_____

_____

_____

_____

_____

A. Write only "Bee humming-bird is 2½ inches."

IV. _____

_____

A. You can review notes at 7:30 P.M., before you go to sleep, or the first thing in the morning.

V. _____

_____

A. Thesis/conclusion system
B. Fact/principle system

VI. _____

_____

Speak Out

In addition to identifying the main ideas during lectures, we must also be able to get the gist of what is said during personal conversations. The main ideas expressed during a personal conversation may be straightforward, uncomplicated statements such as:

I admire my biology professor.

It was fun having the class party at Disneyland this year.

I really don't like dormitory food.

Just as in lectures, this type of statement in conversation is usually followed or preceded by examples and details.

The main ideas expressed during a conversation may not always be so straightforward. For example, the messages that a friend wants you to understand and remember may not be stated directly. The details are given, but a direct statement connecting these details is not given. In these cases, the gist of what the person is saying most often has to do with personal feelings or opinions. Consider this conversation:

Student A: How's the food at the cafeteria here?
Student B: Well, the soup is very salty, they cook the vegetables for hours, and the meat is always gray. If they serve it with applesauce you know that it's pork; if they serve it with mint jelly, it's lamb.

Student B never actually says that the food is terrible, but we know this is how Student B feels; this is the gist of what Student B is saying.

For this activity, you must first speak with a native English speaker who has experienced one of the following situations:

1. attended school in a foreign country
2. lived in a dormitory
3. shared an apartment with other students
4. rented a room from a family
5. taught at a college
6. failed (or almost failed) a class
7. been a member of a fraternity or sorority
8. been active in campus politics
9. worked while going to school

Ask the person to tell you about this situation. Make mental notes of the main ideas. Pay close attention in order to get the gist of what he or she is saying. Then report back to the class about your conversation. Include the following:

1. a brief description of the person you spoke with and the situation you spoke about
2. the main ideas, the gist of the conversation
3. whether the gist of what the person said was stated directly or not

Did any of the people you and your classmates spoke with have similar experiences? Were any of the main ideas they expressed similar? Discuss the possible implications with your classmates.

SKILL B: ASKING FOR CONFIRMATION

Sometimes even when you have heard and understood every word, it is difficult to understand exactly what a speaker means. When this happens, even if you have already asked the speaker to repeat what he or she said, you can ask for further clarification. A good way to do this is to state what you heard in your own words and then ask the speaker if you understood correctly. Obviously, this skill is useful both inside and outside the classroom.

In the classroom, the situation can be sensitive. You don't want the instructor to feel that you think he or she explains things badly. This might make the instructor feel insulted or angry. To confirm that you have understood without insulting the instructor, you must ask your questions carefully. Here are some polite expressions you might use.

One of these:	Followed by one of these:
I'm not sure I understand.	Do you mean that . . . ?
Professor _____, am I (is this) right?	Are you saying . . . ?
I'm not sure I'm following exactly.	Is it . . . ?
I'm not sure I'm getting this.	Do you mean to say that . . . ?
I don't know exactly what you mean.	Do you mean to imply that . . . ?

With friends or family you can confirm something less formally by omitting the first sentence and using only one of the second sentences listed. Or you may simply ask, "You mean . . . ?"

Listen to the following conversations. Expressions to ask for confirmation are used correctly in some and incorrectly in others. Sometimes the *intonation* makes the difference!

Conversation 1

At the side of the road, a lost driver is asking directions from a policeman.

Driver: Pardon me. How do I get to the Schubert Theater?
Policeman: You make a U-turn, go back on Washington until you hit Jefferson, then make a right turn, and it's the second white building on your left.
Driver: Could you repeat that, please?
Policeman: Sure. You make a U-turn, go back on Washington until you hit Jefferson, about three blocks, then make a right turn, and it's the second white building on your left.
Driver: You mean I turn around and stay on Washington until I get to Jefferson and then make a right?
Policeman: Yeah, that's right.
Driver: And did you say it's a white building on the left?
Policeman: Uh-huh.
Driver: Thanks a lot.
Policeman: You're welcome.

This conversation was informal, but still polite.

Conversation 2

Now listen to this conversation between a professor and a student.

Student: I didn't get the directions on your test. That's why I did badly.
Instructor: Well, Tim, the directions say "Answer 1A and then choose and answer 1B or 1C or 1D."

Student: Do you mean to say that we had to do A *and* B or C or D?

Instructor: Yes, you had a choice for the second half of the question.

Student: Oh, okay.

Even though a polite expression is used, the student's voice is impolite. His intonation suggests that he wants to blame the instructor for his own misunderstanding of the directions.

Conversation 3

Here is a similar conversation between the same professor and student.

Student: Professor Thompson, I'm not sure I understand the directions on this test.

Instructor: Well, Tim, the directions say "Answer 1A and then choose and answer 1B or 1C or 1D."

Student: You mean that we all do 1A but then we each could do any one of B, C, or D?

Instructor: That's right, Tim.

Student: Oh, now I see. I won't make that mistake again. Thank you.

This response was polite, even though the student did not use formal expressions. He took responsibility for his own misunderstanding.

Conversation 4

And now a student is talking to a secretary about the preregistration procedure.

Student: What do I do now?

Secretary: You take that white sheet and the blue card. You fill out the white sheet with the courses you want. Then you have your advisor sign the white sheet and the blue card, and you turn them in to the first-floor office in Building Four and pay your fees.

Student: You mean I've got to have my advisor sign both the sheet and the card and then I've got to stand in line again?

Because of his tone of voice and complaints to someone who is not responsible for the situation, this student is rude.

Conversation 5

Compare that last conversation to this one.

Student: Excuse me, could you tell me what I must do next to preregister?

Secretary: You take that white sheet and the blue card. You fill out the white sheet with the courses you want. Then you have your advisor sign the white sheet and the blue card, and you turn them in to the first-floor office in Building Four and pay your fees.

Student: I'm not sure I understand. Do you mean that the advisor must sign both forms? And that I take the forms to Building Four and pay my fees there?

Secretary: Yes, that's right.

Student: Oh, okay. Now I understand. Thank you.

Listen In

Now listen to the lecture again. This time your instructor will stop the tape so that you can ask for clarification. Read the following sentences before you listen to the tape. These are the last sentences you will hear before your instructor stops the tape. Each time the instructor stops the tape, several of you should practice asking for clarification using the appropriate expressions. The first item is done for you.

Stop 1 "One-half of that time was spent listening."
Do you mean that fifty percent of the time was spent listening?

Stop 2 "When we listen, the rate or speed of the message is established by the speaker."

Stop 3 "Actually, people can listen at a rate of 300 words per minute and not lose any comprehension."

Stop 4 "Now he's going to talk about Newton's ideas on motion from Chapter 2 because he's already finished talking about Galileo from Chapter 1."

Stop 5 "Or you may decide to do it the last thing at night before you go to sleep—or the first thing in the morning—after you brush your teeth."

Stop 6 "The thesis/conclusion system works best with well-organized lectures that have an introduction, a body, and a conclusion."

Stop 7 "Then when you review you can see if the principles tie together into one main concept or thesis."

Stop 8 "Believe me, you'll get plenty of chances to practice all of this throughout the term."

Speak Out

Exercise 1 Have you ever given an excuse that was not the truth for something you forgot or did not want to do? Did the other person believe or did the other person question what you said?

Examples:

Student: I'm sorry I don't have my homework, but my dog ate it.
Teacher: I'm not sure I understand. Do you mean to say that your dog likes to eat paper?

Young woman: No, I can't go to the movies with you. I have to wash my hair.

Young man: I don't get it. You mean you wash your hair every night?

Notice the way the teacher and the young man challenge the statements of the student and the young woman. They don't actually say that the other person is lying, but it is clear that they suspect this. By using the expressions for confirming that you have understood and a gentle tone of voice, they may get at the truth and still be polite.

Now, choose a partner for this activity. Make an excuse for something you forgot or don't care to do (for example, returning books to the library, going to the opera, cleaning up the kitchen). You can use something you've actually said before or make up an excuse. Your partner should question the truth of this excuse using an expression asking for confirmation. Then answer the question with another excuse. Your partner should question this, too. Answer with another excuse. Then your partner questions it, and so forth. See how long you can keep making excuses. Then change roles. Later, change partners and try it again. Here's how it might go:

Student: I'm sorry I don't have my homework, but my dog ate it.

Teacher: I'm not sure I understand. Do you mean to say that your dog likes to eat paper?

Student: Well, yes he does, actually—some sort of deficiency, I think.

Teacher: I'm not following this. Are you telling me that paper has nutritional value?

Student: You see, when he was a puppy he was taken away from his mother too soon and . . .

Teacher: Wait—am I right? Do you mean to tell me that you don't have your homework because your dog had an unhappy childhood? . . .

Exercise 2 Do this activity in small groups. Imagine that you have completed your education and have a wonderful job in the research and development department of a large company. The other members of your group work there too. You have just invented a new product. Decide as a group what this is, what it does, how it works, and so forth. Examples:

A wristwatch-t.v. that can be blown up like a balloon to become a ten-inch t.v.

An electromagnetic device that can be attached to your tongue to help you pronounce English perfectly

Next, take turns with the other groups describing your strange but wonderful products. When you are listening, interrupt in order to clarify the descriptions of these unusual items. When your group is speaking, be ready to answer any and all questions about *your* product.

CHAPTER 3
THE FAMILY

All cultures in the world have some type of family system or network. Most sociologists define the family as a group of people related by blood or marriage, who most often live together under one roof. In some cultures this includes the elderly—people over sixty-five. In this chapter you will hear a lecture on family networks and the elderly. The lecture might be for an undergraduate sociology course.

Lecture: Family Networks and the Elderly
Skill A: Listening for Key Terms
Skill B: Making Generalizations
Skill C: Listening for "Straw Man" Arguments
Skill D: Introducing Information

PART ONE

DISCUSSION

As a class or in smaller groups, discuss the treatment of the elderly. The following questions will help guide your discussion.

1. What do you know about the treatment of the elderly in the United States (or Canada)? Do the majority of older people live with their children and grandchildren or by themselves? Do the elderly, in general, live far from or near their children? What distance would you consider far? What distance would you consider near?

2. What do you think the daily life of a sixty-five-year-old person in the United States is like? If you know any elderly people in the United States, describe them. How old are they? What is daily life like for those persons?

3. What is life like for an elderly person in your native country? Include topics listed in Question 1 in your discussion.

4. Would you rather grow old in the United States or in your own country? Why?

VOCABULARY

As you know, many words have more than one meaning. The definitions of the following vocabulary words match the way the words are used in the lecture.

alienated	*to feel removed, not associated with family or friends*
assumption	*an idea that is understood to be correct*
to favor	*to like best*
household	*people living under one roof, often a family living together*
left	*remaining*
network	*a system of connections*

Exercise 1 Complete the following sentences with the correct forms of the vocabulary words.

1. The young boy on the bus gave his seat to the elderly woman because there weren't any other seats _____.

2. The old man felt _____ when none of the young people wanted to listen to his story.

3. There are five people, including a grandparent, in the Smith

   _____.

4. The elderly couple _____ the apartment on the lower floor because it was not easy for them to climb the stairs any more.

5. In many cities there is a _____ of volunteers who provide assistance to the elderly.

6. We shouldn't make _____ that all elderly people are sickly or that all young people are healthy.

Exercise 2   Discuss the following questions.

1. Have you ever felt alienated? If so, under what circumstances?

2. What assumptions did you make about college life before you got to college? How accurate were they?

3. Which would you favor: having all your classes in the morning or in the afternoon?

4. How many people live in your household?

5. How many hours of classes do you have left this week?

6. What network would you use if you wanted to get someone to introduce you to the president or director of your school?

PART TWO

SKILL A: LISTENING FOR KEY TERMS

Terms an instructor *defines* in a lecture are key terms. In almost all of your courses you will learn new terms. In many of your courses you will learn that terms you already know have a more specific, more definite meaning when used by your instructors in the classroom than they do when used by your friends in social conversation. Some terms in a lecture that are new to you will be new to the other students, too. Terms that instructors define in a lecture are either new to most of the students or are used in a new way in the course. These new terms are often used to describe the most important concepts in a lecture. They are usually defined at the beginning of a lecture or when the instructor begins a new topic.

Listen In

The lecture in this chapter is divided into two parts. Listen to the first part now. Listen for the words the instructor defines. Write down any key terms the instructor gives.

Listen to the lecture again. This time, write a brief definition next to each key term. When you have finished, compare your list of key terms and definitions with your classmates' lists.

Key Term	**Definition**
_____	_____
_____	_____

Key Term	Definition
_____	_____
_____	_____
_____	_____
_____	_____
_____	_____
_____	_____
_____	_____
_____	_____
_____	_____
_____	_____
_____	_____
_____	_____

Speak Out

In small groups, describe a typical day at home with your family. In the United States and in Canada this would probably be a Sunday, when most people do not have to work and the children do not have to go to school. Usually your instructor encourages you to use only English during speaking activities, but this time you may use some words from your native language. These words should only be ones that do not translate easily into English or that you can describe, but do not yet know the exact translation of in English. An unusual food or custom, a game, a type of clothing, or an idiomatic expression may be examples of these words.

As you are sharing your typical day at home with your family, be sure to define these words from your native language, these key terms.

As you listen to your classmates, note the words that they define, the key terms. If you don't understand something, feel free to ask them to define it again. You may find the expressions for asking for clarification or confirmation (see Chapter 1, "Skill B," and Chapter 2, "Skill B") useful here.

Key Term	Definition
_____	_____
_____	_____
_____	_____
_____	_____
_____	_____
_____	_____
_____	_____
_____	_____
_____	_____
_____	_____
_____	_____
_____	_____
_____	_____
_____	_____
_____	_____
_____	_____

SKILL B: MAKING GENERALIZATIONS

When we make statements about things that can be counted, we try to be accurate. For example:

> Of the 100 elderly people who were interviewed, 15 preferred to live with their children and grandchildren, 80 preferred to live alone, and 5 did not have a preference.

Sometimes such detailed accuracy is not necessary. At other times we don't actually know the specific details but do have some idea or opinion about what they might be. In these cases we will probably want to describe only tendencies or trends—that is, what we think happens *most* of the time. To do this, we omit any specific statistics and make more general statements. These generalizations are introduced by adverbs of time and expressions such as the following:

by and large	in general
for the most part	normally
generally	typically
generally speaking	usually

Example: By and large, elderly people prefer to live alone.

We can also make generalizations in the negative. That is, we can generalize about what does *not* happen most of the time. To do this, we can simply change an affirmative statement that follows the expression of generalization to a negative one. Another way we can generalize about what does *not* happen most of the time is to omit the expression of generalization and add instead an adverb such as:

hardly ever   seldom   rarely

For example, those two sentences have about the same meaning:

For the most part, rock concerts are not performed in homes for the elderly.

Rock concerts are hardly ever performed in homes for the elderly.

Listen In

Listen to Part 1 of the lecture again. Pay special attention to how the instructor uses some of the expressions listed in the "Skill B" section. Mark the following statements T (true) or F (false) as you listen. When you are finished, compare your answers with those of your classmates. Then listen to the tape as many times as

necessary to check the answers. Then change all the false statements to true ones by using appropriate expressions.

1. _____ People over sixty-five are always called elderly.

2. _____ There are only two types of families: nuclear and extended.

3. _____ By and large, a man and his wife and children are the members of what we call a nuclear family.

4. _____ In extended families, married couples rarely live with their parents.

5. _____ Generally, in Africa and Japan, people choose to live in extended families.

6. _____ In many countries, people generally choose to live only with the nuclear family.

7. _____ One assumption many people make is that, generally speaking, elderly people see their children on a regular basis.

8. _____ Another assumption many people make is that elderly people hardly ever see their siblings.

Speak Out

Divide into groups of five or six. Discuss family life in the United States and in your native country with the other members of your group. You may want to discuss such things as divorce rates, the number of single-parent families, the average number of people in a household, the number of children per nuclear family, the age when people marry, where the elderly live, who is responsible for earning money, who is responsible for household chores. Use appropriate expressions for making generalizations about these topics.

SKILL C: LISTENING FOR "STRAW MAN" ARGUMENTS

If you must fight with someone made of straw, you most likely will win. Thus, a "straw man" argument is an argument that can be defeated easily. Instructors will often use "straw man" arguments in their lectures. For example, they will make a statement from one point of view (the "straw man" argument) and later they will demonstrate why this point of view is not accurate (defeat the argument). Many "straw man" arguments are based on assumptions people have made that are not true. Many professors feel that part of their job is to help students look objectively at their beliefs, the assumptions they might have made.

Listen In

Listen to Part 2 of the lecture. Listen for the "straw man" arguments and why they are untrue. You will probably need to listen to the lecture more than once. Fill in the following chart as you listen.

"Straw Man" Argument	Information Used to Defeat the "Straw Man" Argument
1. _____ _____	_____ _____
2. _____ _____	_____ _____
3. _____ _____	_____ _____
4. _____ _____	_____ _____

THE ELDERLY IN THE UNITED STATES

TABLE 1 ELDERLY LIVING WITH CHILDREN OR WITHIN TEN MINUTES BY CAR: THE UNITED STATES AND SOME EUROPEAN COUNTRIES

Denmark	52%
United States	61%
Great Britain	66%
Poland	70%
Yugoslavia	73%

TABLE 2 FREQUENCY OF ELDERLY VISITS WITH THEIR CHILDREN

Within 24 Hours		Last Week	
Great Britain	47%	Yugoslavia	71%
Yugoslavia	51%	Poland	77%
United States	52%	Great Britain	77%
Denmark	53%	United States	78%
Poland	64%	Denmark	80%

TABLE 3 PERCENTAGE OF ELDERLY WHO SAW A SIBLING WITHIN THE LAST WEEK

Women		Men	
Poland	37%	Great Britain	28%
Denmark	58%	Denmark	32%
Yugoslavia	40%	Poland	33%
Great Britain	41%	United States	34%
United States	43%	Yugoslavia	48%

Adapted from Ethel Shanas, "Family-Kin Netwarks and Aging in Cross-Cultural Perspective." *Journal of Marriage and the Family*, August 1973, pp. 508–509. Copyrighted 1973 by the National Council on Family Relations, Fairview Community School Center, 1910 West County Road B, Suite 147, Saint Paul, Minnesota 55113. Reprinted by permission.

Exercise 1 Divide into groups of five or six. Then choose one of the following questions. It's all right if two people choose the same question. Also, it will be more interesting if you choose a situation that you have not experienced yourselves.

What do you think it's like to:

- grow old?
- be a single parent?
- have teenaged children?
- live with your spouse's parents?
- be married and have no children?
- be married, have small children, and work?
- live alone as a young person?
- live alone as an old person?

Take about two minutes to think about the question you have chosen. Think about what daily life is like for the person in this situation. Because you have not had the same experience, you will have to imagine, to make some assumptions about that person's daily life. Share these assumptions with the rest of your group.

Did anyone in your group disagree with your assumptions? Based on their own experience or on any statistics they might know, could anyone in the group show that your assumptions were not accurate?

Exercise 2 Interview someone in the community who is currently in the situation you selected. Ask about daily life, specifically about some of the assumptions you made. Share with the entire class what happened during the interview. Did any of your assumptions turn out to be "straw man" arguments? Which ones?

SKILL D: INTRODUCING INFORMATION

When we introduce new material or points during a talk, we usually try to prepare the listener in some way. If the point is expected or not likely to arouse excitement, we use expressions such as:

Let's consider . . .
Let's examine . . .
Let's reexamine . . .
Let's look at . . .

If, on the other hand, the point we are introducing is rather surprising, we use expressions such as:

Believe it or not . . .
In fact . . .
Let's face it . . .
Oddly enough . . .
Surprisingly . . .
This is hard to believe, but . . .
You may be surprised that . . .
You may not (won't) believe this, but . . .

In informal conversations, we may use expressions such as these to introduce the surprising points:

Guess what!
Do you (ya) know what?
Surprise!

Listen to the following conversations for examples of expressions used to introduce surprising information.

Conversation 1

Mark: Hey, guess what!
Connie: What?
Mark: You won't believe this, but my grandfather called and said he's just joined an athletic club.
Connie: What's so surprising about that?
Mark: Well, he's eighty-five years old and always hated sports and exercise of any kind as far as *I* know.

Conversation 2

George: Surprise!
Gina: Uncle George, how nice to see you! Where's Aunt June? Isn't she with you?
George: Nope! Believe it or not, she decided to stay home this trip. She always liked the drive up here to see you kids, but I think her arthritis has been bothering her lately, so she decided to stay home.
Gina: Well, you may be surprised to know that I'm old enough to drive now, so maybe my brother and I can come down to visit her soon, okay?
George: Oh, I'm sure she'd love that!

Listen In

Listen to Part 2 of the lecture again. List the points that the instructor thinks are surprising.

_____

_____

_____

_____

_____

_____

_____

_____

Speak Out

Exercise 1   Think of an experience in your family or in someone else's that was unusual because the results were very unexpected. In small groups, share these experiences. Use the expressions in "Skill D" to introduce the surprising points. For example:

> Once my family and I went on a picnic in Golden Gate Park in San Francisco. I put my purse down on the grass. Later on everyone went for a walk. We came back two hours later. Believe it or not, my purse was still on the grass. In fact . . .

Exercise 2   Reporting research. Call a Medicare office, a home for the elderly, a county hospital, or an elderly friend, and ask about benefits for the elderly. Bring your information back to class and share it with the members of your group. Use the expressions in "Skill D" to introduce the surprising points.

CHAPTER 4
HEALTH

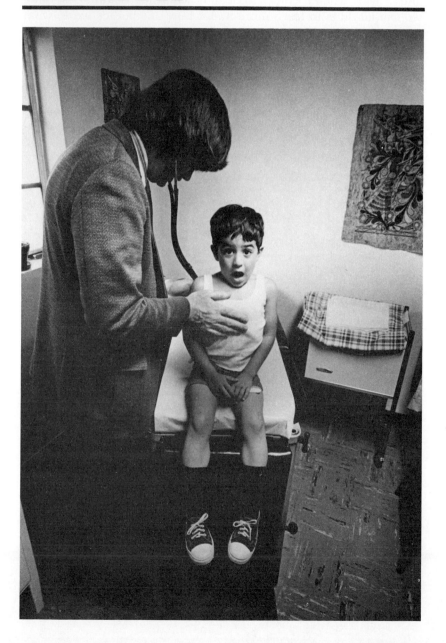

Many people regard good health as their most important personal possession. Knowing that many diseases can be avoided, these people want to know what they can do *now* to stay well. For them, saying "I could have" or "I should have" after becoming ill is not good enough. They are more interested in "I can," "I have to," and "I will" when it comes to dealing with their health. One thing we can all do is to learn more about how our bodies work, what makes us tick. The lecture in this chapter is on cardiac muscle and might be presented in a basic life science or physiology course.

Lecture: What Makes Us Tick: Cardiac Muscle
Skill A: Listening for Analogies
Skill B: Expressing Opinions

PART ONE

DISCUSSION

The human body is often compared to a machine. In what ways is the human body like the machines listed below? Consider specific organs as you discuss these questions.

Example: a camera

The eye is like an automatic camera. It automatically focuses for short and long distances and automatically adjusts for lighting conditions.

1. a car
2. a robot
3. a boat
4. a furnace
5. a computer
6. a telephone switchboard
7. a video recorder
8. a garbage disposal
9. a printing press
10. a telephone answering machine

VOCABULARY

The lecturer in this chapter uses the following words as he describes the cardiac muscles and provides some examples.

chambers   *compartments*
hollow   *having an empty space inside*

overall	in general, including everything
peel	outside covering of some fruits, such as bananas
to pump	to propel or push
strip	long, narrow piece
ticktock	the sound a clock makes
undoubtedly	unquestionably, without any doubt
to vary	to change, differ
canary	a small yellow bird

Complete the following sentences with the correct forms of the vocabulary words.

1. Anthony Robbins, who runs fourteen miles every day,

   _____ has the strongest heart in the class.

2. The _____
   in the heart fill and empty as the heart works.

3. The _____ of the clock reminded Diana of her own heartbeat.

4. Jane's mother bought her a _____ to try to cheer her up after her recent heartbreak.

5. The heart _____ the blood through the body.

6. Ruben's health is, _____, quite good.

7. You can use the _____ of an orange to make some healthy drinks.

8. Francis used a _____ of cloth to make a bandage.

9. The size of an animal's heart _____ according to the size of the rest of the body.

PART TWO

SKILL A: LISTENING FOR ANALOGIES

When instructors explain a new concept to their students, they often compare the new idea to something that is already familiar to them. For example, the human body is said to be like a machine. Or, to take another example, the eye may be said to be like a

47

camera. These comparisons are called *analogies*. Analogies are frequently used to make information clear. The instructor compares something the students are already familiar with to something new. The following expressions are often used when making analogies:

like	the same as
just like	similar to
about the quality (size, color, etc.) of	as

Listen In

Listen to the lecture once all the way through.

Now listen to the lecture again and write down all the analogies you hear. You could write them in a short form, as in the following examples.

Examples: body = machine

eye = camera

_____

_____

_____

_____

_____

_____

_____

_____

How many analogies did you write down? Listen to the lecture once more and see if you can find any more analogies the instructor uses.

Speak Out

You have just heard a lecture that included many analogies. Using analogies in your conversation can make what you say clearer, more interesting, and even poetic. In this activity you will have the opportunity to describe actions, feelings, and objects by making analogies.

Following are several situations. For each situation, think about how people might feel. What are they doing with their hands? Their eyes? Their bodies? What objects are in the situation with them? What things do these situations—feelings, actions, and objects included—remind you of?

With a classmate, choose one of the situations and pantomime it for the rest of the class. Don't talk. Just present a brief silent scene and let your classmates describe your feelings and actions by making analogies. An example is provided for the first situation.

1. *In the dentist's office:* The patient is extremely fearful. The dentist is confident and reassuring.

   While you and your partner are portraying the scene, your classmates might offer analogies about the characters, such as the following:

   The patient:

   His hand is shaking like a leaf.
   His face is white as a sheet.
   His mouth feels just like dry desert air.
   His skin feels cold and damp as a frog.
   His stomach is like a tight fist.
   His heart is pounding just like a hammer.
   His foot is tapping like a woodpecker.
   He feels as scared as a rabbit.

   The dentist:

   He feels as solid as a rock.
   His heart is ticking like a quiet clock.
   He has a smile like a well-fed baby's.
   His eyes are calm, like a lake on a windless day.
   His legs are steady, just like two oak trees.
   His touch is as comforting as a soft blanket.
   His hands move precisely, just like an expert watchmaker's.

2. *In the hospital:* The patient is just waking up after an operation. The nurse is new on the job and taking care of a patient for the first time.

3. *At the health club:* The member did too much exercise on the exercise equipment and is now in extreme pain. The director is nervous because other members might think that there's something wrong with the program or with the equipment.

4. *In the woods:* A couple is backpacking for the first time. It's getting dark, they haven't eaten, it's starting to rain, and they can't figure out how to put up the tent.

5. *At home:* A child who doesn't want to go to school pretends to be sick. The mother knows that the child is not really sick.

6. *At the office:* The boss is giving a long, uninteresting talk on sales data for the month. An employee who should be listening is thinking about an upcoming ski trip.

7. *In the school cafeteria:* Two students are eating lunch.

SKILL B: EXPRESSING OPINIONS

In the lecture in this chapter, the speaker presents a lot of factual information. In addition to these facts, the speaker expresses many personal opinions. In general, when lecturers want to express personal opinions, they use specific expressions to introduce them. These expressions help the listener to distinguish the factual information from information that may be only personal beliefs or ideas. The following expressions may be used to introduce personal opinions:

> I guess . . .
> I imagine . . .
> I personally think . . .
> I strongly believe . . .
> I suspect . . .
> I think . . .
> I'd say . . .
> I'm almost positive . . .
> I'm convinced . . .
> I'm fairly certain . . .
> I'm positive . . .
> I'm pretty sure . . .
> Not everyone will agree with me, but . . .
> To my mind . . .
> Undoubtedly . . .

By using these expressions, speakers can be sure that they will not give listeners misinformation. This is especially important in personal conversations. In most instances we do not want to mislead other people, nor do we want to sound like "know-it-alls"— people who say that *they* know the facts or the truth, but who are frequently proved to be wrong later on.

Listen to the following conversation, in which two people express their opinions.

Conversation 1

Joe: I suspect that heart disease is the number one killer in the United States.
Shmo: No—no, it's cancer.

Joe: Well, I'm almost positive that it's heart disease. Didn't Dr. Strongheart say that . . .
Shmo: Nope—you're wrong. It's cancer.

Here Joe and Shmo both express opinions, but Shmo does not indicate that his is a personal opinion. He sounds like a "know-it-all," and he may or may not be correct. Shmo might remedy the problem like this:

Conversation 2

Joe: I suspect that heart disease is the number one killer in the United States.
Shmo: Oh? I always thought it was cancer.
Joe: Well, I'm almost positive that it's heart disease. Didn't Dr. Strongheart say that . . .
Shmo: Yes, but—not everyone will agree with me—I'm pretty sure Dr. Strongheart doesn't have his facts straight.

Listen In

Listen to the lecture again. This time, focus on the expressions the instructor uses to express opinions. Then read the items below. Each item relates to an opinion the lecturer has. Add the missing information to each item, using your own words if you wish.

Example: The instructor strongly believes that the cardiac muscles are *the most amazing muscles in the human body.*

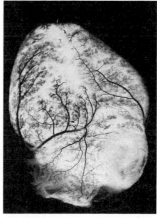

A human heart.

1. The instructor believes it is the action of the cardiac muscles that _____ _____ .

2. According to the instructor, the heart looks like a _____ .

3. As visualized by the instructor, the walls of the heart are about the thickness of _____ _____ .

4. The instructor is pretty sure that if you open and close your hand thirty-eight times in half a minute, your hand _____ _____ .

51

5. The instructor suspects that, generally, a woman's heartbeat is faster than a man's because _____

_____ .

6. The instructor is convinced that we will know more about the

_____

_____ in fifteen years.

7. According to the instructor, your heart works _____

_____ .

8. According to the instructor, the heart rests because _____

_____ .

9. The instructor thinks that one day you will be able to get heart repairs as easily as _____

_____ .

10. Does the instructor believe that everyone will agree with his opinion about heart repairs? _____.

Speak Out

Divide into groups of five to seven for this activity. Discuss the following situations and use the expressions in the "Skill B" section to introduce your personal opinions. Feel free to add other situations for discussion relating to health.

After you have discussed the situations, role-play them as the characters suggested. Divide the roles among the group. If necessary or if you like, add a few characters of your own.

1. The office workers in an insurance company did not do well on the yearly physical examination. They must decide what can be done to improve their physical fitness. They hold a meeting to discuss this.

   Characters to Role-Play:
   the owner of the company
   an extremely overweight secretary
   the company doctor, who smokes
   the company nurse, who is a "health nut"
   a young executive, who jogs to work

2. Should sex education be taught in school? If so, at what level (elementary, secondary, college) and in what class (health,

biology, physical education)? A school meeting is held to discuss this issue.

Characters to Role-Play:

a conservative parent
a broad-minded or liberal parent
a school principal
a high school senior
a counselor

3. Should smoking be allowed in places such as classrooms, restaurants, banks, and other places where the public gathers? How about work places? Do you think the government should be involved in this decision, or should it be left up to the managers or employees or both to decide? A company meeting is held to discuss this issue.

Characters to Role-Play:

an office worker who doesn't smoke but must work in a room with many smokers

a student who enjoys smoking

a pregnant woman who becomes ill at the smell of cigarette smoke

a person with a lung disease

an elderly person who has smoked since the age of fifteen

CHAPTER 5
TECHNOLOGY

Technological advances excite and impress just about everyone. The advances in the area of space technology have been particularly exciting and impressive. The lecture in this chapter might occur during a field trip for a class that deals with any aspect of space technology.

Sometimes an instructor will take students on a field trip to help them see first-hand what he or she has been talking about in lectures. Since the trip is considered a part of the course, notes must be taken. On an exam or quiz, instructors often include questions on information students get during a trip, so we will be taking some notes as we experience a simulated flight into space at the Lyndon B. Johnson Space Center in Houston, Texas. Professor Chapman is leading the trip.

Lecture: Space Flight: A Simulation
Skill A: Taking Notes on a Field Trip
Skill B: Shifting Focus

PART ONE

DISCUSSION

Many people disapprove of spending billions of dollars on space exploration. These people seem to think that there are better things to spend money on. On the other hand, others agree wholeheartedly with the funding of a space program in order to expand human knowledge—not just knowledge about space but knowledge in general.

Divide into two groups for five-minute discussions. Let each group represent one side of the space exploration issue. Group 1 should come up with five problems that they believe governments should solve before any money is spent on space exploration. Group 2 should list five fields of study, unrelated to space exploration, that have been significantly enriched by space programs and space research. Both groups should select a secretary to take notes and report to the class as a whole about what was discussed by their group.

After the secretaries report, take some time to discuss the issue so that you can express your own views (regardless of which group you belonged to) about whether a "superpower" or any other country can afford to fund a space program.

A launching of NASA's space shuttle *Columbia*.

VOCABULARY

The words in the following list are used in the lecture by the guide at the Johnson Space Center.

acceleration	*process of going faster*
altitude	*distance above sea level*
astronauts	*people who fly spaceships*
atmosphere	*air surrounding the earth*
cargo bay	*an area in an airplane or spaceship used to keep cargo, special goods, or materials*
external	*on the outside (opposite of internal, on the inside)*
friction	*the rubbing of one thing against another, resistance to motion by two surfaces that are touching*
to manipulate	*to control*
mission	*job*
navigational	*concerning the control or steering of a ship, airplane, or spaceship*
to orbit	*to travel around a body in space (such as the earth)*
orbiter	*a vehicle or thing that orbits*
remote	*distant, far*

satellite   *an object or vehicle made or built to orbit the earth or another body in space*

shuttle   *(v.) to travel back and forth frequently; (n.) a vehicle used to shuttle*

simulate   *to copy the appearance or effect of something*

solar   *of or about the sun*

Complete the following sentences with correct forms of the vocabulary terms. There may be more than one correct answer.

1. _____ need a lot of training before they can be put in charge of a flight.

2. Although the scientist was on earth and the spaceship was 690 miles above earth, it was his _____ to repair the ship by _____ control.

3. In order to help the average person understand space exploration better, t.v. artists _____ the movement of rocket ships on the t.v. screen.

4. The horrified pilot found it was impossible to _____ the _____ instruments in order to steer the plane.

5. The bombs were held in the _____ of the plane.

6. As a spaceship enters the earth's _____ at an _____ of 400,000 feet, a great deal of resistance or _____ builds up.

7. They shot up a _____ to _____ the moon; the _____ worked perfectly.

8. There is a bus that will _____ passengers from the airport parking lot to the terminals.

9. On the outside of the spaceship you will find _____ panels, which collect the energy from the sun.

10. As the rockets fired, the _____ of the spaceship pushed the pilots into their seats.

PART TWO

SKILL A: TAKING NOTES ON A FIELD TRIP

It is difficult to take good notes on a field trip. Often, so much material is presented that students can become confused. Here are three hints to help you feel more confident about taking notes on a field trip.

1. Obtain as much information as possible about the place you are going to visit before the trip. The more you know, the easier it will be for you to understand what your guide tells you. One good way to get information is to go to the library and look in a recent encyclopedia for the information about the place you are going to visit. Another way is to ask students who have already been on the trip what they learned.

2. Take down numbers. In lectures on scientific topics especially, numbers can be very important. It is often useful to write down a number you hear even if you don't have time to write down all the information concerning the number. You can always go back to the instructor and ask for more information. For practice, read the following numbers aloud:

$$
\begin{aligned}
10 &= \text{ten} \\
100 &= \text{one hundred} \\
1{,}000 &= \text{one thousand} \\
10{,}000 &= \text{ten thousand} \\
100{,}000 &= \text{one hundred thousand} \\
1{,}000{,}000 &= \text{one million} \\
10{,}000{,}000 &= \text{ten million} \\
100{,}000{,}000 &= \text{one hundred million} \\
1{,}000{,}000{,}000 &= \text{one billion}
\end{aligned}
$$

$$
\begin{aligned}
1/2 &= \text{one half} \\
1/3 &= \text{one third} \\
1/4 &= \text{one fourth} \\
1/10 &= \text{one tenth}
\end{aligned}
$$

If you don't hear a number, you can always ask to have it repeated.

3. Get help from and give help to a friend. Of course you won't be able to take down every word, and neither will anyone else. Plan ahead to get together with a friend soon after the trip to go over notes together. If you know before the trip that you will have help after the trip, you can relax and listen well, without anxiety.

So, three hints for note taking on a field trip are:

1. Before the trip, read about the place you are going to visit.
2. During the trip, take down the numbers you are given and ask for repetition of those you don't catch.
3. After the trip, get together with a friend to compare notes.

Listen In

The Johnson Space Center handed out the following diagram of the space mission in which you are about to participate. Look at the diagram and the list of coded headings below it. Before you listen to the tape, can you imagine which of the nine codes go with each of the pictures? Naturally, the headings are not listed in sequence, or order of occurrence. Listen to the lecture all the way through. Label each picture with a code as you listen to the lecture. The first one is done for you.

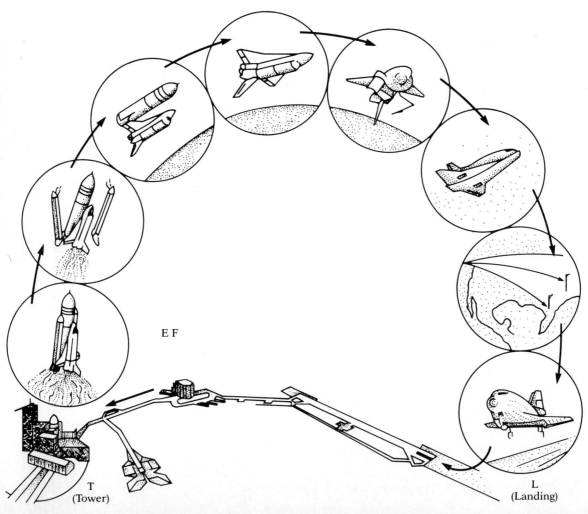

E F

T
(Tower)

L
(Landing)

T   = Tower
CCB = Closing Cargo
        Bay
D   = Deorbit
EF   = Engines Fire
BR   = Booster Rockets
        Drop Away

EO = Enter Orbit (altitude 690 miles)
ET   = External Tank Drops Away
L   = Landing
RMA = Using Remote Manipulation
        Arm

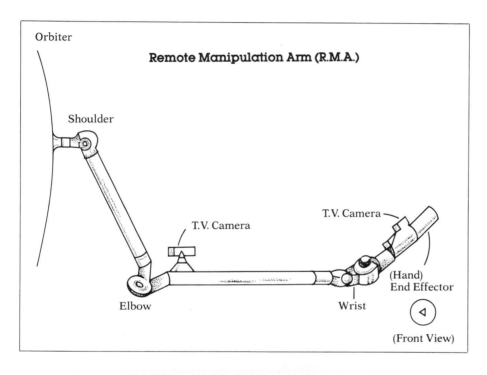

Mission Control at Johnson
Space Center.

Now that you have a clearer idea of the technical vocabulary used in the lecture, it will be easier to listen for numbers and statistics. Read Items 1–10. Then listen to the lecture again and fill in the blanks with the correct figures or other information.

1. The spaceship's acceleration builds up to _____ feet per second as we move away from the earth.

2. The booster rockets use up their fuel and drop into the sea about _____ minutes after takeoff.

3. As the spaceship goes into orbit, its speed is _____ times the speed of sound.

4. When the spaceship is in orbit, it flies at an altitude of _____ miles.

5. The fifty-foot mechanical arm attached to the orbiter is called the _____ .

6. The area where the satellite will be repaired is called the _____ .

7. The shuttle enters the earth's atmosphere at _____ feet.

8. As the shuttle begins to deorbit, or fall to earth, it is _____ miles from its landing site.

9. As the shuttle reaches the earth's atmosphere, the surface temperature of the orbiter can reach _____ degrees Fahrenheit.

10. The tiles protecting the orbiter are called _____ tiles.

Speak Out

Choose a partner for this activity. Then choose a city or town that you are very familiar with and enjoy. Give your partner a "mini-tour" of this city or town while he or she takes notes and asks questions. Here are some kinds of information you might want to include in your tour:

1. points of historical interest
2. shopping areas
3. museums
4. city or town hall

5. tourist attractions, such as amusement parks, zoos, theaters
6. schools and universities
7. geographical attractions (lakes, rivers, mountains)
8. transportation systems

After describing and discussing the town and asking and answering questions about it, class members should be able to make a two- or three-minute report on their partner's favorite city. If you prefer, you may take your partner on a "minitour" of someplace other than a town—for example, a college, a factory, or a resort that you know well.

SKILL B: SHIFTING FOCUS

As you have heard in this and previous lectures, instructors tend to use an impersonal, rather formal English. To create this feeling of objectivity, they often use the passive voice. Since the talk we have just heard is a technical lecture, the passive voice is used frequently. Here are some hints to help you recognize the passive voice and to help you compare it with the active voice.

1. A verb in the passive voice consists of a form of the verb *to be* plus a past participle—for example, *The shuttle was flown.*

2. In sentences using the passive voice, a "doer" is mentioned when the "doer" is important, but the "doer" is not as important as the subject of the sentence. If the "doer" is mentioned, the preposition *by* is used, and the "doer" follows: *The shuttle was flown by my uncle.* The uncle is the "doer," but he is not the focus of the sentence—the shuttle is. Notice the impersonal tone of the sentence.

3. In sentences using the active voice, the "doer" is the subject of the sentence and the focus of attention—for example, *My uncle flew the shuttle.* Notice the introduction of a personal element: *my uncle.* In fact, the speaker could be bragging and stress *my: My* uncle flew the shuttle. The speaker is then definitely involved personally.

Listen to the following conversations. You will hear the active voice contrasted with the passive voice, the personal with the impersonal.

Conversation 1

In a neighborhood front yard.

Mother: Why is the baby crying?
Father: I don't know, but a dog just ran out of the yard.
Mother: There are teeth marks on her arm!
Father: The dog must have bitten her.

Conversation 2

In the police station.

Policeman 1: What was that last phone call about?
Policeman 2: The mother of a small baby was really upset and she wants us to find a stray dog.
Policeman 1: Why? Was there any trouble?
Policeman 2: Yes, the baby was bitten by the dog.

Conversation 3

Husband: What happened?
Wife: The lights just went out!
Husband: What do you suppose is the reason?
Wife: They probably turned off our electricity because we didn't pay our bill!

Conversation 4

Electric Company Official: Good morning. This is the electric company.
Customer: My name is Ellen Bates and my electricity went out last night.
Electric Company Official: Just a minute, Mrs. Bates. I'll check your records.
Customer: Thank you.
Electric Company Official: Ah, yes, here they are.
Customer: What happened?
Electric Company Official: Your electricity has been turned off because your bill hasn't been paid.

Listen In

Look at the following incomplete sentences. Read them to yourself and then be prepared to listen for the complete sentences as you hear the lecture for the third time. The sentences are all in the passive voice and appear in the order of their occurrence in the lecture. Complete the sentences with the correct forms of the verbs in parentheses.

1. "At T minus zero the booster rockets on either side fire,

   and three seconds later we _____ (lift) off the ground by the combined energy of the five engines."

2. "Two minutes after takeoff the fuel in the booster rockets

   _____ (use up)."

3. "Since the failure of its control system, the satellite has been going through space without guidance—going so fast

that it cannot _____ (reach) directly by the remote manipulation arm.''

4. ''The 'hand,' or what _____ (call) the

end effector, _____ (fit) with three inside wires.''

5. ''A short arm of the satellite _____ (catch) by these wires.''

6. ''Remember, we said that the satellite was moving too

quickly _____ (pick up) directly by the RMA.''

7. ''We hear Mission Control Houston through the wall

speakers: 'Your mission _____ (accomplish)!' ''

8. ''We _____ (protect) by thermal tiles covering the ship from surface temperatures of 2750 degrees Fahrenheit.''

9. ''The heat is so great that radio communications

_____ (block) for twelve minutes of our descent.''

Speak Out

Exercise 1 Coastal areas and deserts are often chosen as sites for space centers and bases. With a partner, try to think of at least two reasons for this. Then give your suggestions in the following ways.

1. One partner is the head of Space Administration. You are talking by telephone to the person in charge of selecting the next site for a U.S. space base. Tell him or her where to build the base and why. Use the active voice; you are directly involved.

2. The other partner is a professor telling a classroom of students about the placement of space bases in the United States. Tell them where they are located and why. Use the passive voice; you are not directly involved.

Exercise 2 Radio and t.v. announcers try to remain impersonal and detached from the stories they report; the passive voice is often used in news reporting. Here are some ''facts'' about an imaginary accident at a U.S. space base. Take turns adding a sentence to the report, using the passive voice and the cues provided. Note that

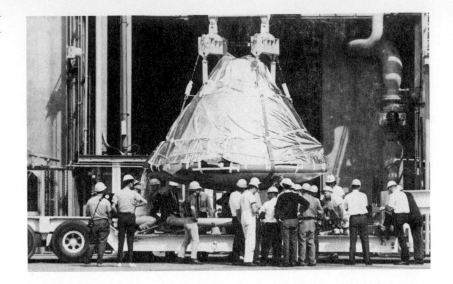

Technicians and officials at Cape Kennedy, Florida, inspect a spacecraft in which three astronauts lost their lives in a flash fire on the launching pad.

the events are in chronological order and in the past. The first item has been done for you as an example. You may add additional items if you wish.

Yesterday there was a tragic fire after a lift-off on launch pad number 2.

1. the astronauts / give

   The astronauts were given their breakfast at 5:00 A.M.

2. the countdown / begin
3. the astronauts / ask
4. the controls / check
5. all systems / test
6. the signal / give

Suddenly a fire broke out in the booster rockets before the spaceship took off.

7. the astronauts' cabin / fill
8. the fire / put out
9. the pilots / kill
10. two mechanics / injure
11. Mission Control / shock
12. burned pieces / find
13. the public / inform
14. the next mission / cancel

Exercise 3 Consider an event that you or someone else in the class experienced or witnessed. Report this event to the class in the style of a news report. You may make this report humorous or serious, as you wish.

CHAPTER 6
MONEY MATTERS

The saying "Neither a borrower nor a lender be" is certainly good advice but very difficult to follow these days. If you want to buy a house or car or send your children to college, you will probably have to borrow money. If you want to start a new business, expand an existing business, or develop a new product, you will probably have to borrow money. Similarly, countries that need to develop their businesses and industries in order to help their economic position in the world also borrow money. In this chapter you will hear about the World Bank, an organization that lends money to developing nations.

Lecture: The World Bank

Skill A: Listening for Pros and Cons
(Arguments For and Against)

Skill B: Agreeing and Disagreeing

PART ONE

DISCUSSION

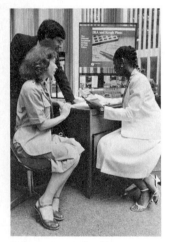

A young couple discusses financial planning with a bank officer.

Banks are often seen as friends in time of need. For instance, when the owner of a small business wants to expand, the local banker may be the first person to see. Or, when a busy salesperson has to replace a car, he or she often rushes to the loan department of the nearest bank. On the other hand, some people think that banks are their worst enemies. One example might be the struggling young family that finds it impossible to pay the mortgage on their home because of illness or unemployment. The bank forecloses and takes away the property. Whether banks are friends or enemies depends on one's point of view. Think of people and businesses you know about that have been helped or hurt by banks. Share these specific examples with your classmates.

VOCABULARY

The following vocabulary items are the words in the lecture on the World Bank that may be new to you.

to borrow	*to take something with permission (with the intention of returning it)*
breeding	*sexual reproduction of animals*
environmental	*relating to the surrounding medium*

to invest	*to put money into a project in order to earn more money*
irrigation	*watering of farmland by canals, ditches, and so on*
to loan	*to give something (with the intention of getting it back)*
proposal	*suggestion*
snail	*a simple animal in a coiled shell*
stock	*shares in a corporate business that can be bought and sold and may change in value from day to day*
waste-water treatment facility	*place where used water is purified*

Use the correct forms of the vocabulary words to complete this crossword puzzle. (Answers are on p. 151.)

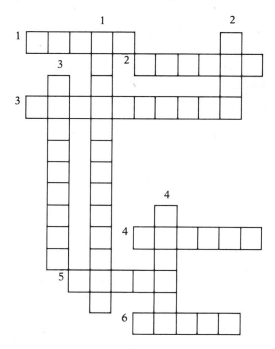

Across

1. Rabbits and mice do this rapidly.
2. What you do when you need money.
3. Dry lands need this in order to produce food.
4. Some people eat them.
5. What is left over and no longer useful.
6. The . . . market went up.

Down

1. Air and water pollution problems are . . . problems.
2. You hope that the bank will . . . you money.
3. What businesspeople often study before making decisions.
4. A banker will tell you how to . . . your money.

PART TWO

SKILL A: LISTENING FOR PROS AND CONS (ARGUMENTS FOR AND AGAINST)

In lectures, instructors often state arguments for and against the points they are making. These are called *pros* and *cons*. The economics professor whom you will hear describes the three member agencies within the World Bank and tells you something about how each one operates. He gives at least one argument pro and one con for each agency. He does this from two points of view—from the point of view of the needy country that the agency helps and also from the point of view of the member agency itself.

In order to point out both pros and cons, the economics professor has to show the listener that he is shifting ideas. He has to use words that indicate a switch. For example, if your investment banker tells you that it is a good idea to invest in a certain company, he will probably add that there are certain risks involved. He might say the following:

> Now is the time to invest in Company X because it is just beginning to grow and it is not yet well known. If, however, it grows too quickly, it would be a good idea to sell within a year.

The word *however* tells you that the banker sees both sides of the matter. He sees the arguments for investing in a growing company, but he also sees the arguments against. Words such as *however* indicate that the speaker is changing his focus or viewpoint. Here are some other words that can serve in the same way:

although
but
however
instead
nonetheless
on the contrary
on the other hand

Listen In

Listen to the lecture once all the way through.

Now listen to the lecture again and fill in the following chart as you listen. Look at the chart before you begin. You will probably need to hear the lecture a few times in order to fill in the chart.

A waste-water treatment plant in Belem, Brazil.

An irrigation project in Madagascar.

MEMBER AGENCIES FOR THE WORLD BANK

International Bank for Reconstruction and Development	International Development Association (IDA)	International Finance Corporation (IFC)
PRO (ADVANTAGE)	**PRO (ADVANTAGE)**	**PRO (ADVANTAGE)**
1. _____	1. _____	1. _____
2. _____	2. _____	2. _____
CON (DISADVANTAGE)	**CON (DISADVANTAGE)**	**CON (DISADVANTAGE)**
1. _____	1. _____	1. _____
2. _____	2. _____	2. _____

71

A speaker at a World Bank conference.

Speak Out

How to best spend and invest money is a problem not only for ministers of finance but for the "little guy" as well. The average person tries to save a certain amount of money every month, and over a period of time money builds up. The question at that point

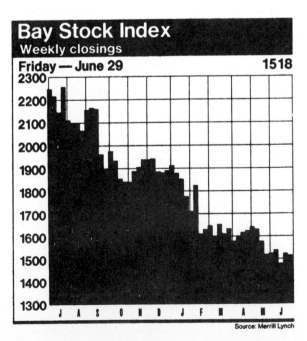

Bay Stock Index
Weekly closings
Friday — June 29   1518

Source: Merrill Lynch

is what to do with the money. Do you stuff it in a mattress for a rainy day (most experts would cry at the thought!) or do you attempt to put your money to work for you so that the amount grows? Here are three possible ways to invest money:

1. Buy a condominium. Rent it now and sell it later at a profit.

2. Buy stocks on the stock market.

3. Put your money into special high-interest bank accounts.

Of course, there are many pros and cons to each of these types of investments.

Divide into small groups and discuss these investments. Try to come up with three or four pros and cons for each type of investment. After you have listed all the pros and cons that you can think of, take a vote on which seems best. Report the results to the rest of the class. Once the class is together again, individual students might want to suggest other investment choices. List on the board all the possible investments mentioned. As each suggestion is made, offer pros and cons.

SKILL B: AGREEING AND DISAGREEING

When instructors give a point of view, they expect students to be able to react to their statements by agreeing or disagreeing. They admire students who are able to express their own points of view. This is considered independent thinking and is valued. Of course, being able to agree or disagree is valuable outside as well as inside the classroom. All of us are called upon daily to give our points of view in conversations with friends, relatives, and acquaintances. To feel comfortable when we make a point, we need to know the vocabulary of agreeing and disagreeing. We need to know which expressions are polite and which are not. The following will acquaint you with a few of these expressions and will help you to decide when to use them. Here are some ways to express agreement:

Informal (to be used with friends)
Exactly.
I'll say!
I knew it!
Okay!
That's right.
That's for sure!
You'd better believe it!
You can say that again!

73

Formal (to be used in situations requiring respect)

I agree.
I agree with that.
I couldn't agree more.
Exactly. (Exactly right.)
That's absolutely true.
That's correct.
That's precisely the point.

Here are ways to express disagreement:

Informal (to be used with very close friends; in other situations, they are likely to seem impolite)

You've got to be kidding!
You've got to be joking!
That's a laugh!
That's a joke!
You don't know what you're talking about!

Formal (very strong expressions to be used in formal situations)

I don't think so at all.
No, definitely not.
I don't agree.
I don't believe that.
I'm afraid not.
You couldn't be more wrong.

Polite Formal (to be used in situations requiring respect)

That's more or less true, but . . .
I guess that's true, but . . .
I understand what you mean, but . . .
Yes, but isn't it also true that . . .
I guess you could say that, but . . .

Listen to the following conversations, in which expressions of agreement and disagreement are used both correctly and incorrectly.

Conversation 1

In a college classroom, a student is challenging an instructor.

Instructor: And furthermore, it is my contention that had it not been for aid from neighboring countries, the war would have been lost.
Student: You've got to be kidding! Military planning was the key!

This response is rude.

Instructor: And furthermore, it is my contention that had it not been for aid from neighboring countries, the war would have been lost.

Student: Yes, but isn't it also true that excellent military planning helped?

This is an appropriate response.

Conversation 2

In the school cafeteria, two students are chatting.

Student 1: Corned beef hash again! The only time we have anything decent to eat is when the parents visit!

Student 2: That's precisely the point!

This response is too formal.

Student 1: Corned beef hash again! The only time we have anything decent to eat is when the parents visit!

Student 2: You can say that again!

This is an appropriate response.

Conversation 3

At a business executive meeting, two board members are discussing future plans.

Board Member 1: It's obvious that if we don't branch out and get into other areas of interest, eventually the company will fail.

Board Member 2: I don't believe that! We must cut costs.

This response is too strong.

Board Member 1: It's obvious that if we don't branch out and get into other areas of interest, eventually the company will fail.

Board Member 2: That's more or less true; however, I think that by cutting our costs we can accomplish a great deal.

This is an appropriate response.

Conversation 4

At the doctor's office, a doctor and her patient's wife are discussing the patient.

Doctor: Mrs. Franklin, your husband has a variety of medical problems and it's absolutely essential that he get more exercise and lose at least twenty-five pounds.

Mrs. Franklin: I knew it! He's too fat.

This response is too informal.

Doctor: Mrs. Franklin, your husband has a variety of medical problems and it's absolutely essential that he get more exercise and lose at least twenty-five pounds.

Mrs. Franklin: I couldn't agree with you more, Dr. Lewis. I've been trying to get him to diet for years.

This is an appropriate response.

Listen In

Listen to the lecture again. This time your instructor will stop the tape occasionally so that you can have the opportunity to agree or disagree with the lecturer. Have the list of expressions from the "Skill B" section in front of you so that you can express your points of view politely and formally. When you agree with a point, support your idea with an example from your own experience. When you disagree, give your reason. Go over the following sentences before listening to the tape. They will be the last sentences you hear before your instructor stops the tape, so it is important that you understand them thoroughly. The first item is done for you.

Stop 1 ". . . Industry couldn't afford to be charitable."

Agreement: **That's absolutely true. It was the same way in my hometown when the air pollution got so bad. Many businesses looked elsewhere for locations.**

Stop 2 "In general, you could say that a broad industrial base leads to economic success."

Stop 3 "The bank asked environmental consultants to consider the consequences of the new irrigation system because it's true that technological advances often add significantly to environmental problems."

Stop 4 "Once a medical scare is introduced, it is extremely difficult to prove that a program, project, or product is 100 percent safe."

Stop 5 "The more international contact a country has, the greater the opportunity for economic success."

Stop 6 "Some say the best loans have no strings attached."

Stop 7 "Nonetheless, we all know that it is difficult to separate economic goals and political interests in today's world."

Speak Out

Exercise 1 Divide into two groups. Go over the following information about the nearly bankrupt country of Almost Broke. Then describe at least five steps that could be taken to improve its economic condition and report your suggestions to the other half of the class. The class members from the other group should say whether they agree with the proposals or not and why. Be sure to begin with the expressions of agreement and disagreement presented in this chapter. It would be best to begin with formal expressions. Then, since you know your classmates rather well, use the stronger, less polite expressions if you wish.

The Land of Almost Broke

abundant natural resources
   (recently discovered): oil,
   uranium
a common language (spoken
   by all)
several large towns
several large rivers flowing
   from the mountains
a large lake
a pleasant climate
a mountainous central region

landlocked (no outlet to the sea)
only one major export
imports greatly exceed exports
high unemployment rate
high illiteracy rate
high inflation rate
poor soil
a large population
a low hourly wage
unfriendly neighbors

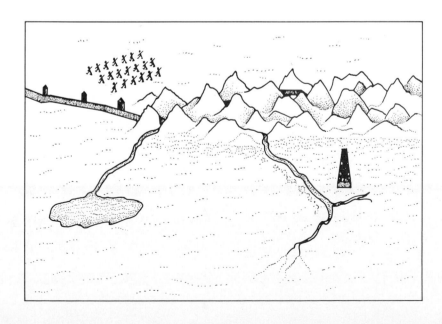

Exercise 2   Bring to class a newspaper or magazine article with which you strongly agree or disagree. Summarize the issue for the class, state the author's point of view, and explain why you agree or disagree. As you are not speaking directly to the author, you may use the stronger, less polite forms of disagreement. The formal forms are preferable to the informal because you are in a structured situation: the classroom. Remember, you will need to use the third person when you speak about the author. For example, instead of "You couldn't be more wrong," say "He couldn't be more wrong."

CHAPTER 7
LEISURE TIME

Scientists and researchers from many backgrounds are interested in the relationship between work and leisure time and how this relationship affects daily life. Historians, sociologists, psychologists, economists, and anthropologists, to name a few, find the subject fascinating. The lecture in this chapter might be a part of a series of lectures on work and leisure time for a college sociology class.

Lecture: Leisure Time in Our Society
Skill A: Listening for Chronological Order
Skill B: Expressing Likes and Dislikes

PART ONE

DISCUSSION

The lecture mentions that, in today's technological society, holidays tend to commemorate political rather than religious events. Of the main holidays in the United States for which we get a day off work, only two are religious in nature. Which are they? Is this true for you and your family: Are the majority of the holidays your family celebrates secular rather than religious? Make a list of holidays that people in the class celebrate. Discuss the two holidays

the most people in the class celebrate and the two least frequently celebrated holidays. Discuss people who might work on these holidays and why they work.

VOCABULARY

You will hear the following words in the lecture. Look them over and use the following exercises to help you remember them.

aggressively	*forcefully, energetically*
aspect	*appearance of something from one viewpoint*
to convert into	*to become, change into*
counterpart	*equivalent, similar type*
distinction	*difference*
to evolve	*to develop over a long period of time*
notion	*idea*
perspective	*view, viewpoint*
to pursue	*to follow, chase*
saint	*holy or godly person*
textile	*cloth*
trend	*tendency*

Exercise 1 Match the following words without looking at the definitions.

1. _____ to pursue   a. appearance from
                                   one perspective

2. _____ aspect   b. to develop slowly

3. _____ to convert into   c. idea

4. _____ counterpart   d. forceful

5. _____ notion   e. tendency

6. _____ saint   f. difference

7. _____ trend   g. holy person

8. _____ to evolve   h. cloth

9. _____ distinction   i. equivalent

10. _____ aggressive   i. to chase

11. _____ textile   j. to change into

Exercise 2 Now, in small groups, return to your discussion of holidays, days off from work. Take turns saying a sentence or two on the topic. Use at least one of the vocabularly words during each of your turns. Remember: Using a word in conversation today is the best way to remember it tomorrow.

PART TWO

SKILL A: LISTENING FOR CHRONOLOGICAL ORDER

Chronological order is a method of organization based on time. In its simplest form, chronological order takes the reader or listener from a point in the past to a point closer to the present or to the present itself. History is often written in simple chronological order. However, most lectures are more complex than just a presentation of facts or ideas in chronological order. The following lecture is a good example of the way chronological order serves as the foundation for a complex presentation of facts. However, in order to compare present-day ideas of leisure with those of the past, the instructor moves forward and backward in time.

A lecturer frequently uses chronological order as a method of organization because it is easy for students to follow—*if* they know the cue vocabulary. The lecturer uses this vocabulary to lead them from one point in time to another.

Take note of the following expressions that indicate time or sequence. They will help you understand the instructor's train of thought and whether the facts are presented in simple chronological order (from past to present) or not.

after	later
afterward	next
before	now
by . . . (time)	past
during	present
eventually	presently
finally	recently
first	soon
formerly	then
from . . . to . . .	today
in . . . (date)	until
in . . . (adjective) times	while
last	

Listen In

Look at the following chart and statements before you listen to the lecture. When you are sure that you understand the chart, start to listen. As you listen, decide on the time frame for each statement and indicate it with an *X*. In one case you will need to mark more than one time period for a statement. The first one has been done for you.

Statements	Prehistoric Times	4th Century: Roman Times	13th Century: Medieval Times	1700s–1800s: Industrial Age	1900s: Present Times
1. Workers begin to punch time clocks.				✕	
2. Workers see no distinction between work and play.					
3. Workers pursue leisure time aggressively.					
4. The 2,000-hour work year is common.					
5. The work week of the common worker begins to increase.					
6. Workers are relatively affluent.					
7. The term *worker* includes many categories.					
8. The word *worker* referred to clerical workers and skilled craftsmen and excluded common laborers and women.					
9. Holidays are more likely to be named after presidents than saints.					
10. Labor unions argue that a worker's birthday should be considered a holiday for that worker.					

After punching in at the time clock, workers place timecards in the rack.

Speak Out

In order to keep track of time sequence in a lecture, a student not only must be aware of vocabulary indicating chronological order but must also follow the logic of the given information. For example, before a person can begin to write, it is understood that he or she must pick up a pen or pencil. In addition to common sense, word repetition, the use of pronouns to refer to previously mentioned nouns, and the choice of a definite or indefinite article can give clues to chronological order. Which of the following sentences would come first? Second? Third? Why?

The bus stopped in front of her.

Marcia was waiting for a bus.

Eventually Marcia reached her destination.

Here is a game that will make you think about chronological order and logic. In groups of five or six, use the following sentence as a story starter. After one student has read the starter and added another sentence to it, a second student takes over and continues the story. Go around the group this way until every student has had two turns. The last student must, of course, finish the story.

Look at the words from the "Skill A" section as you play the game. Use as many of them as you can.

Story Starter Sentence: Since this was the first day off that nurse Jane O'Brien had had in over a week, she had intended to put her feet up and enjoy a good book, but that was not what happened!

Now start a few stories of your own. Stay on the topic of leisure time as much as possible, but the setting and details are up to you.

SKILL B: EXPRESSING LIKES AND DISLIKES

Everyone has likes and dislikes, and you will frequently find yourself in situations in which you have the chance to express them. A variety of expressions can be used for this purpose. The nature of the situation (whether it's formal or informal, for example) must be considered before choosing which expression to use. Also, even in very informal situations the feelings of others must be considered. They might like something very much that you do not like at all. If you are going to make a statement indicating dislike, you might want to use an expression that would soften it—make it less strong. In most situations, the way to make a statement less strong is to introduce it with a gentler expression, one that is softer than you would normally use.

Also, as with many expressions in English, you must be aware of your tone of voice. When choosing between making a gentle or a strong statement, your tone of voice can be more important than the actual expression you choose.

The following expressions are some of the most common ones used for expressing likes and dislikes. They are listed in order from the least strong to the most strong. In situations in which it is best not to be outspoken, the strongest statements will not be appropriate.

Here are some ways to express likes.

I like . . .	This is my idea of . . .
I enjoy . . .	I'm tickled by . . .
I'm pleased by . . .	That's terrific/great/super!
I'm happy to . . .	What a terrific/great/super . . . !
I appreciate . . .	I love . . .
I'm delighted by . . .	

Here are some ways to express dislikes.*

I don't especially like . . .	. . . is more than I can stand.
I don't care for . . .	I can't take/stand/bear . . .
I dislike . . .	What a rotten . . .
I don't have time for . . .	I abhor . . .
I can't tolerate . . .	I hate . . .
. . . irks me/bugs me. (informal)	

Listen to the following conversations expressing likes and dislikes. The first one takes place during a job interview.

---

*All of the affirmative expressions of likes can, of course, be put into negative forms to express dislikes.

Conversation 1

Interviewer: I'm happy to say we have quite a good recreation program for the employees.
Prospective Employee: Now this is my idea of a job!
Interviewer: Ah . . . yes . . . , well, we have a gym with exercise equipment to use before and after work or during the lunch hour.
Prospective Employee: I can't stand that kind of exercise!
Interviewer: Oh?

You may have guessed that our prospective employee would not get *this* job. Now listen to a similar situation.

Conversation 2

Interviewer: I'm delighted that you're interested in the company recreation program.
Prospective Employee: Oh, yes. I really enjoy getting to know my coworkers in more informal circumstances.
Interviewer: Well, we have a bowling team that gets together every Friday evening.
Prospective Employee: I don't really care for bowling. Are there any other sports that the employees do as a group?
Interviewer: How about softball—or bicycling?
Prospective Employee: Yes, I enjoy bicycling. That would be nice.

Now compare the next two conversations between friends.

Conversation 3

Rafael: Hey, want to go to the concert with me on Saturday?
Ana: Oh, no, . . . I abhor that kind of music.
Rafael: Oh, well, I thought you might like it.
Ana: No, I don't have time for that sort of thing.

If we speak to our friends in this way, we might not have them for long. Here's a better way to handle this sort of situation.

Conversation 4

Rafael: Hi—how about going to see that new play at the experimental theater tonight?
Ana: Thanks, but I don't especially like that type of theater.
Rafael: Oh, gee—I thought you would.
Ana: No, I dislike it because I don't usually understand what's happening.

Listen In

Listen to the lecture once or twice to get the main ideas. At several different points the lecturer expresses a like or a dislike. The lecturer also asks the class a few things about *their* likes and dislikes.

Listen to the lecture again. This time, jot down on the following page all of the lecturer's likes and dislikes that you can. Later, compare your notes with those of your classmates.

Most Americans have two weeks of paid vacation a year.

87

_____
_____
_____
_____
_____

When the lecturer asks a question about your likes or dislikes, stop the tape and answer it before listening to more of the lecture. Practice using the expressions in "Skill B" to express your likes and dislikes in response to these questions.

Speak Out

Exercise 1 Look over the following chart of leisure-time activities. Circle those things that you really enjoy and make an X through the ones you do not like very much. Add other likes and dislikes in the blanks. As a class or in smaller groups, discuss why you marked your charts the way you did. Use expressions in "Skill B" as necessary to express your likes and dislikes.

DO YOU LIKE OR DISLIKE . . . ?

Art	Sports	Food	Music	Television	Dancing	Reading	Other
art museums	jogging	Japanese	rock 'n' roll	old movies	rock 'n' roll	newspapers	_____
photo exhibits	tennis	Mexican	classical	soap operas	ballet	novels	_____
international crafts	weight lifting	Italian	jazz	news	tap	magazines	_____
natural history museums	skiing	American	New Wave	cartoons	toe	short stories	_____
painting	bicycle riding	Indian	soul	documentaries	jazz	textbooks	_____
ceramics	judo	Chinese	rhythm and blues	weekly comedy series	modern	poetry	_____
_____	_____	_____	_____	_____	_____	_____	_____

Exercise 2 Do this activity in groups of five or six. As you consider each of the following situations, think about what you would say to the person in the situation and to a friend with you. Take turns in your group making these statements. Notice the differences in the choice of expressions and tone of voice, depending on whom you are speaking to. Some examples are provided for the first situation. Note that often we express dislikes to strangers by describing something that we like as an alternative.

1. A man sitting in front of you at the movie theater has three noisy children with him. They are throwing popcorn at each other and talking too much. You have already asked the father politely to do something about the situation, but there has been no change. It's time to take stronger action.

   To the father: I really appreciate a quiet theater.
   (*Or:* I really don't like all this noise.)
   To your friend: Let's move; I can't stand this.

2. You are a single woman out with your woman friends at a bar. You are enjoying yourself, and you do not want the company of a man this evening. However, a certain man has been staring at you. He is definitely not your type, and you do not even want to speak to him. However, here he comes. . . . Your response:

   To the man: _____

   To your friend: _____

3. For several years you have been eating at a local restaurant. The food has been good, the atmosphere pleasant, and the service friendly and attentive. Lately, however, things have changed. The new waiters don't seem to care about you, the restaurant doesn't seem as clean as before, and the food is often mediocre. You have decided to give the restaurant one last chance, and as you are eating a tasteless stew, the owner approaches you and asks you if everything is all right. Your response:

   To the owner: _____

   To your friend: _____

4. You have enrolled in a real estate class in your spare time. Unfortunately, the instructor often digresses from the subject at hand by telling long and uninteresting stories about his travels. You want to spend your time learning more about real estate. Your statement:

   To the instructor: _____

   To your friend: _____

5. You have become involved in a local project attempting to find jobs for teenagers. However, lately the supervisor has asked you to give more time by doing some door-to-door soliciting for funds. You have already given what time you can, and you have said that you aren't interested in this approach, but the supervisor has continued to insist that you help. Your statement:

To the supervisor: _____

To your friend: _____

CHAPTER 8
CREATIVITY

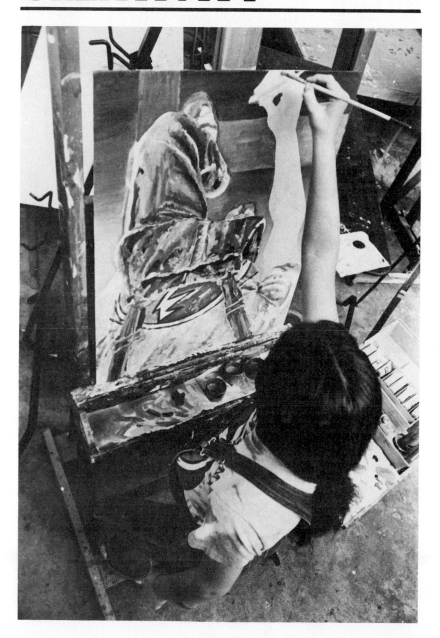

Is creativity an inborn gift, like being athletic or handsome? Or is it something that can be acquired, like money or knowledge? Are only those people called artists truly creative? Or can engineers, biologists, taxi drivers, and waitresses be creative too? What is the nature of the creative process and why does this process seem to reach a dead end at times? These are a few of the questions that will be touched upon in this chapter on creativity.

Lecture: The Creative Process:
  As Fundamental to the Engineer As to the Artist
Skill A: Listening for Signal Words
Skill B: Divulging Information

PART ONE

DISCUSSION

Exercise 1   Being creative is not limited to scientists or artists; for instance, it is carried on all the time by amateur inventors who find new and more convenient ways of doing everyday things. For example, the paper clip was invented by a man who kept losing his paperwork. Besides being a millionaire, he is now very well organized!

Discuss the following list of inventions and describe how they

An unique invention for commuting.

represent creative new ways of doing everyday things. In your discussion, you might consider first the things they replaced.

1. typewriter
2. adding machine (calculator)
3. lightbulb
4. solar heating
5. ballpoint pen
6. refrigerator
7. rubber band

Exercise 2 Often we are unable to see the potential uses for familiar things. In small groups, take an ordinary object such as a rubber band, a ballpoint pen, or a safety pen. Look at it closely for a brief time and make a list of ten things you could do with it (aside from its normal use, or course). Share your findings with the group.

Exercise 3 Here's another group activity to stimulate new thoughts. Sit in a circle if possible. Take any ordinary object you see around you: a cup, a leaf, a pencil, a sweater. Give the object you have to the person on your left, and take the object from the person on your right. Now, let your thoughts flow as freely as you can about how the object you are now holding represents your personality (or the personality of someone you know or someone famous, living or dead). Try to think of at least five examples and share these with the group. For instance: A leaf . . .

1. can be very fragile and so am I at times.
2. can be very strong and durable and so am I at times.
3. goes through many changes in its lifetime and so do I.
4. is flexible and bends easily and most of the time I do, too.
5. just hangs around and I like to do that, too.

VOCABULARY

The following words from the lecture point to key aspects of the topic of creativity. Learn the words by studying their meanings and filling in the blanks in the following sentences.

analytical	*referring to close examination of something*
to circumnavigate	*to go completely around something*
fragmentary	*broken into parts*
to fuse	*to bind together*
to inhibit	*to block or frustrate*
original	*unique, the first one of its kind*
solution	*answer to a problem*
specialize	*to limit to a very narrow area of use or study*

Fill in the blanks with the appropriate form of the vocabulary word.

1. If you have a very _____ mind, you will tend to examine both objects and issues very closely.

2. Ferdinand Magellan was the first man to

   _____ the earth.

3. Emotions will often _____ clear thinking.

4. Intense heat may _____ the nuclei of two atoms.

5. He couldn't find a _____ to the problem, probably because his knowledge of the subject was

   incomplete and _____.

6. If you _____ too much in any field of knowledge, you will tend to lose sight of its relation to other aspects of life.

7. To develop your own identity, you can't always imitate

   others; you have to be _____.

PART TWO

SKILL A: LISTENING FOR SIGNAL WORDS

We use signals all the time to communicate our needs and wants. When a child points to an ice cream cone through a store window, for example, he or she is signaling a desire for something sweet. We encounter signals constantly in both words and images when we drive. Without them, driving would be far more dangerous than it is.

In speaking and writing, we often use signal words to prepare our audience for what is to come, what our next idea will be. This allows the audience to listen more effectively. Listening for signal words is especially important when attending a lecture because it aids us in taking notes. If an instructor says, "Now I'm going to outline today's subject for you," we know to prepare ourselves to do outlining. If he or she says, "Now I'm going to review yesterday's material," we know to think about the topic covered the day before and perhaps to look back over our previous notes. Signal words prepare us for what is going to happen next and what we need to do in response. Here are some verbs that serve as signal words that you might hear in a lecture:

analyze	go on (with)
answer	go over
consider	illustrate
continue	justify
criticize	list
define	outline
describe	pick up (where we left off)
discuss	reiterate
emphasize	repeat
evaluate	review
explain	summarize

Listen In

Listen to the lecture once all the way through to get the main idea.

Then listen again, keeping in mind the signal words that have been listed for you. Every time you hear one of these words, note it down in the space provided on page 96. Listen until you have found at least six signal words.

Now listen to the lecture again. This time pay special attention to what comes after each signal word. Imagine that you are in a lecture hall listening to this lecture and taking notes. In the blanks provided beside the signal words you have picked out, note briefly what these words prepared you for. In other words, what did the lecturer actually do after the signal word? If the lecturer has used the signal word effectively, your answers will include a definition or synonym for this word as well as an indication of its specific application in this lecture. The first three are done for you.

Georges Seurat used dots of color to create his impression, *Sunday Afternoon on the Island La Grande Jatte.*

95

Signal Word	What Comes Next; What the Lecturer Does
Continue	*goes on with the discussion of the creative process*
pick up where we left off	*begins with idea started at the end of the last class*
analyze	*examines closely various aspects of the creative process*

Dot puzzle.

Speak Out

Exercise 1 We have been discussing the way signaling occurs in language. But other kinds of signaling go on all the time among human beings, animals, insects, plants, and even individual units of life called cells. For example, cells send chemical messages to one another; plants use pollen, scent, and insects to send messages; birds use markings—or color of their feathers—and sound. It is only with the higher mammals and humans that signals occur in so complex a form as a language.

Below are some animals and insects that are well known for their ability to signal and communicate. Form a small discussion group with your classmates. Each person can take one of the animals listed and, after some brief research, describe to the others the major ways that the animal or insect communicates. How do these animal and insect forms of communication compare in terms of creativity with human communication?

1. whales
2. porpoises
3. monkeys
4. mockingbirds

5. ants
6. dogs
7. bees
8. cockroaches

Exercise 2   Give a solution to the following thought problem: If you were placed in a cell with another person and not allowed to speak or write, what methods would you devise to communicate with the other person?

Exercise 3   Human beings use more than language to signal each other. Two nonverbal signals that people use every day—often unconsciously—are tone of voice and body language. Tone of voice tells us how people really feel despite their words. Body language is another sure indicator of how people really feel. As people's moods change, their bodies assume different positions and postures to reflect those changes. If you are alert, you can read deeper meanings into the words people say by noticing the tone in which they speak and their posture, gestures, and other body language while they speak.

To get a feeling for nonverbal communication, push back the desks (if possible) and form a large circle with your classmates and instructor. Take turns saying an insignificant sentence to someone across the room from you. Your instructor or a classmate will suggest an adjective to describe your attitude as you say the sentence. When it is your turn, take a few steps, perhaps as you say the sentence, to get your whole body into the act and not just your face and voice. Here's a sentence you can use, or you can make up some of your own if you prefer.

Apples are red and bananas are yellow.

Here are a few adjectives to get you started. Add as many as you can to this list.

angry	frightened	murderous
delighted	frustrated	rushed
disgusted	grieving	sarcastic
flirtatious	inhibited	shy

SKILL B: DIVULGING INFORMATION

To divulge means "to give out or disclose." In colloquial English, if someone is divulging information, the implication is that we are being told "the real stuff," "the inside information," "what is really happening." Information that is *divulged* is of a different quality from other information that is given out during a conversation or a lecture. It is important in note taking and outlining that you recognize when information is being *divulged,* because it might be this information that you will be expected to take most seriously and that you will probably be tested on.

When a lecturer is about to divulge something, he or she usually announces this intention—another example of the use of signal words. By now it should be clear that the more you understand about signal words and phrases, the better you will be at picking out information that is important to learn and remember. The following phrases are often used when divulging information:

Despite what you may believe . . .
Despite what you may have heard . . .
Here's how it really is. . . .
The real story is . . .
What's really going on here is . . .

The following slang phrases might be used when divulging information in very informal situations:

The real scoop is . . .
What really gives is . . .
What's really cooking is . . .
Where it's really at is . . .

Note: Most of the preceding phrases can be used in question form in order to ask someone to divulge information.

Listen to the following conversations, which present examples of ways to divulge information. The first conversation is somewhat formal.

Conversation 1

Albert: Did you hear that Professor Finster resigned from his post as president of the Institute of Reverse Psychology?
Bonnie: Yeah. I heard that story, too.
Albert: Why do you say it's a story?
Bonnie: Because I've heard what's really going on. The real story is that he was forced to quit—fired, in fact.
Albert: No kidding—why?
Bonnie: Despite what you believe about him, he doesn't do very careful research and publishes inaccurate data.

Now listen to this conversation, which contains some slang phrases to divulge information in both statement and question form.

Conversation 2

Kate: Hey, what gives? That's a really fine motorcycle Jules is riding. Where'd he get the cash?

Doug: I don't know.

Kate: Oh, come on—what's the scoop?

Doug: Well, he says he saved up for it, but the real story is: He won the money gambling in Las Vegas and he doesn't want his folks to find out.

Kate: I thought he told Susie that he couldn't stand Las Vegas.

Doug: Well, despite what you may have heard, the real scoop is that he's been sneaking off to Las Vegas just about every other weekend.

Listen In

Listen to the lecture again. Pick out the phrases that signal that information is about to be divulged. Write them down in the spaces provided.

Victor Vasarely inventively used curved lines and bars of black and white to create *Zebras.*

Phrases the Lecturer Uses When Divulging Information

1. _____

2. _____

3. _____

4. _____

5. _____

Now listen to the lecture again. Is the information that the lecturer divulges in this way critical to the main points of the lecture? Why or why not? Discuss this with your classmates.

Speak Out

Look at the following incomplete conversations. Only the first line or two of dialogue is provided for you. Choose a partner and together complete as many of the conversations as you can in the time you are given. Use as many of the expressions for divulging information as you can. Then select the conversation that you and your partner enjoyed doing the most and present it to the rest of the class. You might want to take notes on the lines provided.

1. **A:** What's up? I hear Frank's moving to Toledo.

   B: Nah, _____

   _____

   A: _____

   _____

   B: _____

   _____

   etc.

2. **A:** I don't understand this at all. Helen tells me one thing and Jean tells me another. What's going on?

   B: _____

   _____

   A: _____

   _____

   B: _____

   _____

   etc.

3. **A:** I can't get my experiment to work. I've looked in the text-book, but the procedure described there is quite different from the one the instructor described in class.

B: _____

_____

A: _____

_____

B: _____

_____

etc.

4. **A:** Hey, what gives? I thought you'd gotten an A in that class. Paul says that you really knocked his socks off with your last creative writing project.

B: _____

_____

A: _____

_____

B: _____

_____

etc.

5. **A:** Where do you think I should exhibit my paintings? Henry suggested the gallery over by the museum, but Vicki said that only tourists go in there. So that's not where it's really at any more, right?

B: _____

_____

A: _____

_____

B: _____

_____

etc.

6. **A:** Hey, I thought this was supposed to be a surprise party! If we arrive at 6:00, won't he already be there? What's the scoop?

B: _____

_____

A: _____
_____

B: _____
_____

etc.

CHAPTER 9
HUMAN BEHAVIOR

Most of our lives are spent interacting with other people: working, playing, eating—and even in our dreams we interact with others. It's no wonder that people are interested in learning more about how they relate to other people. An academic discipline that studies people and their interactions is called social psychology. In this chapter, a social psychology lecturer examines how people behave in groups. This area of study is called "group dynamics."

Lecture: Group Dynamics
Skill A: Recognizing Digressions
Skill B: Understanding and Using Tag Questions

PART ONE

DISCUSSION

Whenever you are with one or more other people, you are in a group. Think about where you were, what you did, and who you were with for the last twenty-four hours. Fill in the following chart.

Time	Were you alone?	If not alone, number of people you were with	Activity
1 hour ago	_____	_____	_____
2 hours ago	_____	_____	_____
4 hours ago	_____	_____	_____
6 hours ago	_____	_____	_____
8 hours ago	_____	_____	_____
10 hours ago	_____	_____	_____
12 hours ago	_____	_____	_____
14 hours ago	_____	_____	_____
16 hours ago	_____	_____	_____
18 hours ago	_____	_____	_____

Time	Were you alone?	If not alone, number of people you were with	Activity
20 hours ago	_____	_____	_____
22 hours ago	_____	_____	_____
24 hours ago	_____	_____	_____

Share with your classmates how many hours you were alone, how many hours you were with others, and what kinds of groups you were in. Was this a typical day for you? Are people in the class similar or different in the amount of time they spend alone or in groups? Would you prefer to spend more time, less time, or the same amount of time in groups? Why?

VOCABULARY

The italicized words in the following sentences are used in a similar context in the lecture. Below each word are three definitions. Choose the definition that best fits the word as it is used in the sentence.

Example: What's his *field?*

    a. _____ a piece of land with no trees

    b. _X_ a division of academic study

    c. _____ a place where oil is found

1. Joe feels his position as president of a political group on campus is an important part of his *identity.*

   a. _____ individuality, the condition of being oneself

   b. _____ intellect, intelligence

   c. _____ innocence

2. A number of *random* events contributed to Joe's joining the group.

   a. _____ chance

   b. _____ classical

   c. _____ cheap

3. Joe can *pretty much* do what he wants because he shares an apartment off campus and has plenty of money.

   a. _____ never

   b. _____ hardly ever

   c. _____ almost always

4. To some people, *eye contact* is important when speaking to someone.

   a. _____ looking directly into someone's eyes

   b. _____ agreeing with someone

   c. _____ knowing someone's eye color

5. Before Joe can go fishing with his friends, he needs to *wind* his new string around the pole.

   a. _____ to blow

   b. _____ to plant

   c. _____ to wrap

6. Joe took five minutes at the end of a group meeting to *recap* (recapitulate) his ideas.

   a. _____ to change

   b. _____ to bottle

   c. _____ to summarize

PART TWO

SKILL A: RECOGNIZING DIGRESSIONS

Most lecturers digress from time to time. That is, they go off the topic. They do this for several reasons. For instance, a lecturer might want to share an interesting idea that does not relate directly to the subject but that he or she believes the students will find informative or amusing. Another reason for digressing is to connect something abstract to real experiences that are familiar to the students. A third reason for a digression is to help students become more involved in a particular topic. In this case, a lecturer might suggest activities or readings students can do on their own. A final reason lecturers might digress is that they know students cannot maintain intense concentration for the whole class period. Thus, to give students the chance to relax for a few minutes, they go off the subject and then come back to it. When lecturers digress too much, however, it is difficult for students to follow a lecture!

Most lecturers are careful to point out to students when they begin to digress — that is, which material is of secondary importance. (Digressions are unlikely to be tested on an exam.) Sometimes a lecturer begins a digression by announcing it with an apology or request for permission.

In such cases, the speaker may use one of these expressions:

If I may digress . . .
If I may stray from the subject . . .
If I may wander . . .
Let me digress . . .
Let me mention in passing that . . .

Some other expressions that announce digressions are the following:

(Just) As an aside . . .
By the way . . .
Oh, I forgot to mention . . .
Oh, that makes me think of . . .
Oh, that reminds me . . .
Oh, yes . . .
To change the subject . . .
To get off the topic for a moment . . .
To go off on a tangent for a minute . . .
To wander for just a moment . . .

When the speaker returns to the topic, such expressions as the following may be used:

Anyway, as I was saying . . .
As I started to say . . .
Back to our main topic . . .
To come back to what I was saying . . .
To continue with our main point . . .
To get back to the topic at hand . . .
To go on with what I was saying . . .
To return to what I was saying . . .
Well, back to business . . .
Well, back to work . . .
Well, to continue (with the main topic) . . .

Listen In

Read the statements below, which are taken directly from the lecture. Make an educated guess about which statements relate directly to the main points in the lecture and which statements are digressions. Mark the appropriate column to the right of the statement as you decide. The first one is done for you.

How many of the items did you guess were digressions?

		Main Point	**Digression**
1.	"This afternoon I'm going to talk to you about a topic that affects every person in this room: group dynamics."	✓	
2.	"Today we're going to look at . . . patterns of communication in groups and then at how the group affects individual performance."		
3.	"You all went to discussion section yesterday, didn't you?"		
4.	"It doesn't seem to matter how large the group is—only a few people talk at once."		
5.	"Two people do over 50 percent of the talking in any group."		

According to the lecturer, these racers perform better with an audience present.

6. "I must comment here that all the research I know about has been done in the United States and Canada."

Main Point   **Digression**

_____

7. "The research shows that in groups of eight or more, people tend to talk to the people sitting across the table from them."

_____

8. "It seems to me that where I come from we have a social rule that doesn't make much sense."

_____

9. "If you're planning to be a match-maker and start a romance be-tween two of your friends, don't seat them next to each other at your next formal dinner party."

_____

10. "The research also shows that, in general, the person in the group who talks the most is regarded as the leader of the group."

_____

	Main Point	**Digression**
11. "The theory behind this type of research—research that demonstrates that people do better work in groups—is called 'social facilitation theory.'"		
12. "In this matter of having an audience, we're like a number of other creatures."		
13. "As I mentioned earlier, there is also research that demonstrates that individuals perform worse, not better, on tasks when other people are there."		
14. "If you can manage it, you should take tests on a stage with a group of people who are also taking the test in front of a large audience."		

Now listen to the lecture one or more times as necessary. As you listen, determine which of the statements above are introduced by expressions indicating a digression. Write each of these expressions on the line provided after the appropriate statement.

Now turn back to the "Skill A" section. Listen to the lecture again and check off the expressions the lecturer uses to return to the main subject of the lecture. Does the lecturer always use these expressions or does he sometimes digress or return to the subject without using any of them? If so, what does he or she do instead?

Speak Out

Exercise 1 Get permission to sit in on a class that interests you or to attend a lecture that is not part of a course, such as a public lecture on campus, at the public library, at a church, at a museum, or a meeting that is open to the public (for example, a meeting of the Sierra Club). Your local newspaper will list lectures that are open to the public. If it is not possible for you to attend a lecture, listen to a lecture on television or radio—public broadcasting stations frequently provide lectures on current events or interesting historical topics.

Listen for the digressions in the lecture. When you hear one, make a note of the phrase used to introduce it and the reason for the digression: to relax the audience, to keep the audience interested, to provide additional information. Be careful; don't confuse digressions with examples. Report your findings to your class and compare notes. How many digressions did each person hear? What is the average number of digressions per lecture heard by the class members? What was the most frequent reason for a digression? The least frequent?

Exercise 2   Since you don't usually lecture to your friends, informal conversations are often one digression after another! Actually, this applies to most informal situations—with friends, acquaintances, or relatives. As a class or in small groups, discuss the following.

1. In your culture, are there any circumstances in which a digression would be impolite? Are there any circumstances in which it would be impolite *not* to digress?
2. What are some specific reasons people might use digressions in your culture?
3. In what circumstances do you think digressions are most useful?

Exercise 3   Break into groups of five or six to discuss the following activities that we do in groups. In your discussion, get off and back onto the topic as frequently as you can, using the expressions for introducing and concluding digressions from this chapter. You may wish to add some activities to this list.

dating
eating out
going to the movies
investing money as a group
having a picnic
playing a team sport
sharing a dorm room or apartment
studying in a group
working on a team project

SKILL B: UNDERSTANDING AND USING TAG QUESTIONS

Tag questions are common in lectures and conversations. Tag questions are questions added or "tagged on" at the end of a statement. They are very short, usually consisting of only a subject and an auxiliary verb (and also the word *not* when the tag question is negative).

If the statement is negative, the tag question is always affirmative. For example:

      negative   affirmative
He's not coming to soccer practice today, is he?

If the statement is affirmative, generally the tag question is negative:

    affirmative   negative
He's coming to soccer practice today, isn't he?

But sometimes an affirmative statement is followed by an affirmative tag question. For example:

    affirmative   affirmative
He's coming to soccer practice today, is he?

Basically, tag questions are used for three purposes:

1. As genuine questions—the speaker sincerely wants to know the answer. The genuine tag question has rising intonation.

2. As rhetorical questions—the speaker knows the answer (or thinks he does) and just wants confirmation or agreement from the listener. The rhetorical tag question has falling intonation.

3. As "challenging questions"—the speaker uses an affirmative statement followed by an affirmative tag question to signal a challenge meaning "You're (he's, she's) not going to get away with that!" The challenging tag question has rising intonation, but it rises more suddenly than the genuine question.

Intonation plays a big part in conveying the intention of a tag question. The first two examples of tag questions might be genuine questions with rising intonation. These same tag questions could easily be changed to rhetorical questions by using falling intonation. Try it.

The third example is a challenging question (an affirmative statement with an affirmative tag question) with a sudden rising intonation.

There are also a few common expressions used to form tag questions that do not have a subject and a verb. These one-word tags are:

Okay?
Right?
Huh?

Okay? and *Right?* are used as genuine questions. *Huh?* when used as a tag question is always rhetorical. *Huh?* is very informal and should be used only with close friends or family. It is impolite, for example, to use it with teachers or employers.

Finally, there is an idiomatic expression that is often used as a tag question: *Don't you think?* For example, "He plays a fine game of tennis, don't you think?"

Listen to the following conversations, which include tag questions.

Conversation 1

Steven is telling Tom about the first soccer practice of the season, which is only two days away. He isn't sure whether Tom can make it on such short notice.

Steven: Our team is having the first practice of the season this Saturday morning at eight. You'll be there, Tom, won't you?
Tom: Oh sure! I'll be there early.

Now consider this situation. Steven and Tom have been looking forward to playing soccer on Saturday all week. Steven is telling a third friend, George, about the practice. Steven then asks Tom if he's coming, but he asks the question only to confirm what he already knows.

Steven: Our team is having the first practice of the season this Saturday morning at eight, George. You'll be there, Tom, won't you?
Tom: Sure will.

In a third situation, the soccer practice has been arranged for 6:30 A.M. because another team has reserved the field for 8:30. Tom and Steven are talking about Karl, who told Tom that he wouldn't be coming until eight.

Tom: Steve, Karl told me he can't come to soccer practice until eight.
Steven: What a drag. He's always late. He thinks he's coming at eight, does he? Well, I think he's off the team then. He can't come and go as he pleases and still be on the team.

Conversation 2

Now consider this situation. Charlie's boss expects a report on Friday but realizes that it would be useful at the meeting he's going to on Wednesday.

Boss: Charlie, I've got an unexpected merchandising meeting this week. The report won't be done by Wednesday, will it?
Charlie: Well, I don't think so, but we'll work on it.

Conversation 3

Josie comes home and sees Peter, one of her housemates, sitting in the living room with his feet up. Since it's already six o'clock, she concludes that it's not his turn to cook.

Josie: Hi, Pete. How are you?
Pete: Fine, how 'bout you?
Josie: Good. You're not cooking tonight, huh?
Pete: You got it. It's Barry's turn, right?
Josie: I think so, but he's going to be late again, I know it.
Pete: I think so, too. Let's start the soup, OK? Otherwise, it'll be nine o'clock before we ever get anything to eat.
Josie: Okay, you're right and I'm starved. You cut the carrots and I'll do the potatoes.

Listen In

Listen to the lecture again. This time, notice the tag questions. As you listen, fill in the following chart. The first one you will hear is done for you.

	Genuine	**Rhetorical**	**Challenging**
Affirmative	_____	_____	_____
	_____	_____	_____
	_____	_____	_____

The lecturer claims that even ants are more productive in the presence of their peers.

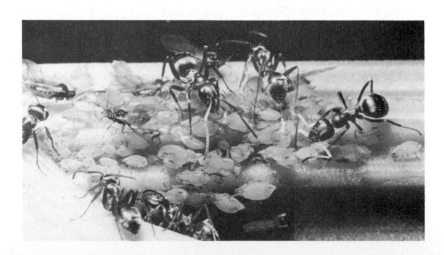

114

Cliff Robertson in *Charlie*, the poignant science fantasy about using drugs to increase intelligence, eyes his opponent and wonders who will win the maze race this time.

	Genuine	Rhetorical	Challenging
Negative	_____	_____	_____
	_____	_____	_____
	_____	_____	_____
	_____	_____	_____
Idiomatic	*right*	_____	_____
	_____	_____	_____
	_____	_____	_____

Compare your chart with those of your classmates. If there are differences, listen to the lecture again and see if you can agree this time.

Speak Out

Native English speakers tend to use tag questions much more than nonnative English speakers. Do the following activities to practice getting confirmation using tag questions.

Exercise 1 In groups of five to ten, get confirmation from one person at a time about his or her leisure activities. For practice, use only statements followed by tag questions to do this. If you are unsure or if you really have no idea what this person does during his or her leisure time, make an educated guess followed by a genuine tag question (with rising intonation). If you definitely know one of this person's leisure-time activities, you may make a statement followed by a rhetorical tag question. When this person has answered all of the tag questions the group can think of on this topic, it's time to get confirmation from another member of the group, and so on. Here are a few examples:

1. You like to play handball, don't you?

    or

    You don't like to play handball, do you?

2. You're a terrific dancer, aren't you?

    or

    You don't like to dance, do you?

3. Your collection of jazz records is the largest in your city, isn't it?

    or

    You don't collect jazz records, do you?

Exercise 2   In groups of two to four, role-play the following scenarios or devise some scenarios of your own. Use as many tag questions—and types of tag questions—as you can during your role-plays. Then present your role-plays to the class. See which group uses the most tag questions, and which group uses the most types of tag questions. To keep track of the scores, you might want to put a chart on the board like the one you used in the "Listen In" exercise and have your instructor or a student volunteer write in the tag questions as they are used in each role-play. You might also give bonus points for using challenging tags in the role-plays, as these can be tricky to use appropriately.

Scenarios

1. At a concert with friends during intermission, half of the group thinks the concert is awful and wants to leave; the other half thinks it's wonderful and wants to stay.
2. A teenager who was supposed to be home by midnight arrives home at 3:00 A.M. The teenager doesn't want to be "grounded" (a punishment in which the young person can't leave the house except to go to school), so he or she tries to tiptoe quietly into the house. One of the parents, however, has come downstairs for a snack and they bump right into each other.

3. At a restaurant, some friends are deciding whether to split the bill equally, have each person pay exactly his or her share, or let one person have a turn paying the whole thing.

4. On your vacation you take an airplane to _____. You try to start a conversation with the attractive person next to you, but a naughty child is making a lot of noise and keeps interrupting you. The parent doesn't seem to be anywhere around.

5. You and some friends are on a mountain camping trip. Although you had planned to stay for five days, it's starting to snow on the second day.

6. At the office, the boss has suggested a ten-hour day, with a four-day work week. The employees may make the final decision, but some of them like to have long weekends, and others prefer to spread out their leisure time over the entire week.

7. At home, you've just received a phone call saying that you've won an all-expenses-paid vacation to Hawaii. You may bring one friend. Your two best friends were sitting with you when you received the call.

CHAPTER 10
CHOICES

Every day, all over the world, people try to discover what they want from life. They try to make choices that will get them what they want. But do we really ever choose anything, or does it only appear that we do? The lecture in this chapter is titled "Choice: The Uniquely Human Problem." In it the lecturer will present an analysis of this intriguing philosophical issue.

Lecture: Choice: The Uniquely Human Problem
Skill A: Paraphrasing
Skill B: Expressing Hopes and Desires

PART ONE

DISCUSSION

The following questions are about personal choices. Break into small groups. Since some of your responses might reflect cultural differences, try to get into a discussion group with students who have different cultural backgrounds from yours. If possible, the ages of the group members should be varied, too. Then answer these questions as honestly as you can.

1. If you could have any kind of job, what would it be? Never mind what you *can* do. What do you *want* to do? Be specific.

2. In which areas of your everyday life do you feel you have the most freedom to make choices (work, school, lifestyle, clothes you wear, food you eat, money you spend, leisure time)? In which areas do you feel you have the least freedom to make choices? Why?

Take out a sheet of paper. Jot down at least six things in life that make you unhappy—for example, you're not getting along with a roommate, someone in your family is ill or has a problem he or she wants you to help solve, your car breaks down often and you can't afford a new one—whatever. Then analyze what you have written in the following way. Divide your list into two parts: (1) things that you *can* control and (2) things that lie within the control of others (or fate or circumstance).

Now look at the two lists. Are the "uncontrollable" things in the second category *really* beyond your control or power to change? What changes could you make to get more control over your life? Write a few specific suggestions. Share your list and your suggestions with the people in your group. Perhaps they can help you find ways to gain more control over circumstances in your life that make you unhappy.

3. What questions about life are you seeking answers to? Discuss at least two. For example:

   a. Why is there so much suffering in the world?
   b. Is violence just part of human nature?

How do you think the way people respond to these questions affects the way they make choices?

VOCABULARY

Exercise 1 To introduce you to some of the concepts used in the lecture, rewrite the following sentences in your own words. Do not use your dictionary; try to get the meaning from the sentence and make an educated guess. Then compare your answers with your classmates'; you may want to check in a dictionary if there are important differences among the answers.

Example: "The unexamined life is not worth living."

If you don't look closely at your own behavior, your life will be meaningless.

1. A philosophical dilemma can probably never be resolved.

   _____

   _____

2. Our lives may be predetermined by our genetic makeup.

   _____

   _____

3. The determinists may be correct in their view, but we still appear to make choices.

   _____

   _____

4. The Eastern concepts of karma, the law of cause and effect, and reincarnation or rebirth epitomize the idea that we are responsible for everything we are and will be.

   _____

   _____

5. Our attitudes toward ourselves and others are often unconsciously conditioned by an underlying philosophical view.

   _____

   _____

Exercise 2 Match each of the following vocabulary words with the best definition. Then write sentences using these words. If you like, you may include more than one of the words in each sentence.

1. _____ abound   a. ordinary

2. _____ condemnation   b. disapproval or criticism

3. _____ criteria   c. to be great in number

4. _____ mundane   d. standards for judgment

5. _____ violation   e. infraction, illegality

PART TWO

SKILL A: PARAPHRASING

In the first vocabulary exercise in this chapter, you were asked to rewrite sentences in your own words. We call this *paraphrasing*, and it can be a useful study skill. In almost every class you are asked to restate in your own words something the instructor said or that you read in your textbook. In an economics course, for instance, you may have read a chapter on economic recessions and depressions. Your instructor wants you to be sure that you understand the difference between these two terms, so he or she may ask you to explain them. When you give such an explanation using your own words but based on what someone else has said or written, you are paraphrasing. Paraphrasing is similar to summarizing, but a paraphrase is about the same length as the original material; a summary is much shorter than the original material.

Listen In

Listen to the lecture once all the way through for the main ideas.

Then listen again and paraphrase the following sections. Your teacher will stop the tape after each section, but you still may want to jot down a few notes to help you remember the ideas presented.

1. Listen closely to the section about Hindu and Buddhist beliefs in karma and reincarnation. Both of these views are said to have important psychological consequences. The key words to listen for are: *pessimist, optimist, choice.* Now paraphrase this section.

At the center of the Buddhist Wheel of Life are anger (snake), greed (pig), and ignorance (rooster), which serve as the basis for unenlightened human choices.

_____

_____

_____

_____

_____

2. Listen carefully to the views presented on decisions involving criminal offenses. An example is given of a judge sentencing a person to prison for violation of certain rules in a community. Now paraphrase this section.

_____

_____

_____

_____

3. Listen carefully to the series of questions faced by most of us presented toward the end of the lecture. These questions refer to the important choices we make. Now paraphrase this section.

_____

_____

When you have finished this exercise, listen to the whole lecture once again to check your work. Then share your work with your classmates by reading it aloud. How did your paraphrasing differ from your classmates'?

Speak Out

You may have heard this quotation: "You can never say 'yes' to something without saying 'no' to something else." Real-life situations often force us to make unpleasant choices and to give up things we want.

Find a partner or partners for this activity. Close all books except one per group. Only one person may look at the textbook. The person with the book will read one of the following items to himself or herself first. Then he or she will paraphrase it aloud for the others. The other students will listen to the situation and make a choice. Discuss the reasons for your choices. Pass the book around so that all students have a chance to paraphrase an item as well as make a choice.

1. You're having dinner with an American family. Everything goes well until they bring in the main course: pork chops with apples. You don't eat pork. Would you:

   a. tell them you're not hungry
   b. explain why you don't eat pork
   c. eat the meal
   d. other

2. You wish to do something about the overpopulation of the world, so you join an activist group that believes:

   a. parents should be voluntarily sterilized after having two children
   b. abortion should be easily available to anyone who wants one
   c. other

3. You wish to end a relationship with someone you have been dating steadily for the past two years. How will you do it?

   a. make a telephone call
   b. meet for dinner one last time
   c. avoid answering your phone for a month
   d. other

4. You have only one parent and she is getting very old and senile. You also have responsibilities to your spouse and children. What would you do?

    a. make arrangements to have mother live in a nearby nursing home

    b. invite her to live with you and your family

    c. other

5. The subject matter for a course you are taking is extremely difficult. Your friend, who took the same course last semester, says that the final is absolutely impossible but that you might pass it with a little "help"—that is, if you are told what will be on the test. Would you:

    a. let your friend give you the answers to the test

    b. let your friend give you some hints but not tell you all of the answers

    c. not accept any help from your friend

    d. other

6. You work in a large computer corporation and are in charge of hiring new employees. You must choose a new office manager from two candidates. One is a long-time friend who is new to the company; the other is a first-rate worker who has been with the company for eight years. You:

    a. offer your friend the position

    b. offer the proven employee the job

    c. other

SKILL B: EXPRESSING HOPES AND DESIRES

The lecturer in this chapter wants students to seriously consider the choices they make and the underlying philosophical basis for these choices. He emphasizes certain expressions, such as *I hope, what if, I wish, if only, I could do with, all I really need is,* and *I could use* to exemplify words we use in decision-making processes. Listen to the following conversation, which includes expressions of hopes and desires.

Laura: Have you found a house to rent yet?
James: No, not yet. I certainly hope I find one soon. My family is arriving in a few days, and I want to have a house ready for them when they get here.
Laura: Sounds like you could use some help.

James: Well, maybe a little, but probably all I really need is more money. If only I didn't have to find something inexpensive. I wish I were making a bit more money. Then I would have a wider choice of houses.

Laura: I wish I could help you with that, but what if I at least help you look in the newspaper for houses and show you where they are on the map?

James: Thanks! That would be great, but I hope it won't be too much trouble.

Laura: No, no! Don't be silly. It's my pleasure!

Listen In

Read the following items before you listen to the lecture once more. Then listen for the expressions in the lecture and complete the sentences.

Use your own words to paraphrase the lecturer.

1. The lecturer *hopes* you remember _____

_____ .

2. He also *hopes* to present more ideas on _____

_____ .

3. *What if* our lives are _____

_____ ?

4. When our bodies need protein and iodine, we *could do with*

_____ .

5. If a lawyer can prove "temporary insanity," he can *hope* to

_____ .

6. All the _____ and _____ are rooted in what we choose to do now.

Complete these sentences with personal information.

7. I wish I were _____ .

8. All I really need is _____ .

9. If only I had _____ .

10. I want to make better choices in my life. I hope to do this by

_____ .

Speak Out

Exercise 1 Situations often come up in which you must express your hopes and desires or ask for what you want. This sometimes requires care on your part, for you do not want to appear impolite. Role-play the following situations to practice these skills.

1. You have signed up for a course that you've been hoping to take for a long time, but you just haven't had the time or the money to do it until now. The instructor begins the first day by asking you to tell him or her what you hope to get from the course. Act this out with a partner: One of you is the teacher and the other, the student.

2. Lucky you! You have been selected for a job interview for a position as a translator at the United Nations (or a job of your choice). The interviewer (your partner) asks what you hope to gain from your experience as a translator and you answer. Then ask the interviewer what qualities he or she hopes to find in an employee.

3. Your friend is twenty-three years old today, and you are planning a surprise birthday party. Your guests will arrive at 6:00 P.M. It's 5:30 P.M., and you realize that you have no ice. You run to your nearby supermarket to get the ice. Unfortunately, there are ten people in line ahead of you. It looks like you're going to be late for your own party. What might your hopes and wishes be in this situation? Turn and express your thoughts to the person in line next to you.

Exercise 2 Charles Burke is on trial for murder. He grew up in a small town in Ohio and then went to Kent State University for one year. When he was nineteen years old he was drafted into the army and was sent to fight in Vietnam. Two years later he returned home and tried to pick up where he'd left off, but things were never quite the same again for Charles. He was expelled from school for fighting with a professor and then was fired from one job after the other. He wanted to meet someone nice and get married, but he just couldn't seem to get close to anyone. He was consumed by anger and loneliness. Finally one day Charles shot someone for no apparent reason. Charles's attorney hopes that Charles will not be held responsible for this crime. He hopes that the judge and jury will understand that Charles was "temporarily insane" and did not really *choose* to commit murder. In a small group, with each person taking a different role, express the wishes and hopes of the various characters in this drama.

Characters

Charles Burke
the defense attorney
the prosecuting attorney
the judge
a member of the jury
Charles's mother (or father)
Charles's best friend from school
Charles's kindly grade-school teacher

In addition to *I wish* and *I hope,* you will want to use the following expressions to help state the sentiments of these people:

If only . . .
I/He sure could use . . .
I/He could do with . . .
All I/he really need(s) is . . .

Exercise 3   Share your responses to Questions 7 to 10 in "Listen In" with your classmates. Were your responses to these items different from the ideas you expressed during the opening discussion for this chapter? If so, in what way(s)?

CHAPTER 11
THE PHYSICAL WORLD

In the wide variety of ecosystems of the world, the polar regions may be unique. Only the hardiest forms of life can survive in these vast icy deserts. In the lecture in this chapter, you will learn more about one part-time polar dweller—the penguin—and the ecosystem in which it lives.

Lecture: The Niche Penguins Have in a Polar Ecosystem
Skill A: Outlining
Skill B: Stating Reasons

PART ONE

DISCUSSION

Imagine yourself in the following situation: You are a zoologist about to embark on a study of penguins. To prepare for your field study, which will include a trip to the polar regions, consider the following questions:

1. What facts about penguins would you want to learn to prepare for the trip?
2. Who would you take with you and why?
3. What supplies would you need?
4. Where would you go first? Why?
5. How would you get to your destination?
6. How much time do you think you would need?
7. What are the dangers you would face?
8. At what times of day would you make your observations? Why?

Test your knowledge of the vocabulary words italicized in the following sentences. They will appear in the lecture. If the italicized word is used correctly, mark the sentence C. If it is used incorrectly, mark the sentence I. The first two items are done for you.

1. __C__ Because I like *desolate* places, I'm thinking of becoming a hermit and moving to an arctic region.

2. __I__ Inland in arctic regions you can find beautiful *beachfront* property.

3. _____ *Catastrophic* floods could change the biological patterns of the world.

4. _____ Most *migratory* birds cannot fly.

5. _____ The term *ecosystem* refers to a network of relationships among organisms that are interdependent.

6. _____ A temperature of 32 degrees *Fahrenheit* is 0 degrees *Celsius*.

7. _____ Birds that *fast* cover a lot of territory in a very short time.

8. _____ Once penguin chicks begin to hatch, the colony begins to *teem* with life.

9. _____ The penguin's *disposition* is black and white.

10. _____ A *ferocious* attack by a sea leopard might kill a penguin.

11. _____ The *brooding* instinct is very strong in penguins.

12. _____ Penguins *engage* in playful activities.

PART TWO

SKILL A: OUTLINING

Information can be condensed and organized for further study by being put into an outline. Outlining is a visual representation of the main ideas and supporting information of a selected topic or text, whether it is a written text or a spoken text such as a lecture. Following is a typical outline format.

I. _____

   A. _____

   B. _____

II. _____

   A. _____

   B. _____

III. _____

   A. _____

      1. _____

      2. _____

   B. _____

This format can vary, depending on the organization of the material. However, the main points are always represented by roman numerals (I, II, etc.), and less important points are represented by capital letters (A, B, etc.) Minor points are represented by arabic numerals (1, 2, etc.).

Listen In

Listen to the lecture on penguins. Pay special attention to the information about mating habits. You will outline this section of the lecture. Part of the outline has been done for you. Fill in the missing information. It is standard practice in an outline to begin each category with a capital letter and to omit end punctuation.

I. Mating habits of penguins
   A. Need for order leads penguins to build nests in rows
   B. Order is often interrupted by small "wars" between males

      1. _____

      2. _____

   C. _____
   D. Losers move to edge of nesting ground

Compare your outline with a classmate's. Check points that you consider important. Ask your instructor any questions you may have about content or outlining. The next task is to construct your own outline.

Listen to the lecture again. Pay special attention to the information about penguin brooding. The following information should be included in your outline of this part of the lecture:

reasons for high casualty rate of eggs
what happens when chicks hatch
cooperative parenting activities

Construct your outline in the space below.

II. Penguin brooding

Speak Out

In the ecosystem discussed in the lecture, penguins are lucky in one way. Their major enemy, the sea leopard, does not use high technology to hunt them. This is not true for many creatures that people hunt. For example, the use of high technology to kill whales has caused worldwide controversy. Answer the following questions with your classmates and teacher.

1. Why are whales hunted? What parts of the whale are used?
2. What methods are used to hunt whales?
3. What is Greenpeace? What does it do?

Now decide what your position is on the following issues.

1. Are the methods used to hunt whales acceptable or not?
2. Should governments control the way in which whales are hunted? The way in which all creatures are hunted?
3. Should whales and other endangered species be protected?
4. Do you support the philosophy of Greenpeace? Its methods?

Present your views to your classmates and explain why you feel this way. A brief outline will help you to organize your thoughts. The major ideas will be your positions on the issues listed (roman numerals), and the less important points will be information to support your position (capital letters, arabic numerals).

The Greenpeace boat *Zodiac* approaches a Soviet whaler in an effort to stop the killing of sperm whales.

SKILL B: STATING REASONS

The lecturer in this chapter has used certain words to emphasize the reasons for the existence of particular patterns and habits of the penguin. These words are also commonly used in everyday conversations for the same purpose. Here are some examples:

because (of)	on account of this	since
for this reason	in view of that fact	seeing as how
the reason is (that)	owing to	(very informal)

Listen to the following conversation, which contains ways to state or give reasons.

Sarah: Hello?

John: Hello. Sarah? This is John.

Sarah: John! Hello! How nice to hear from you. I thought you'd left to do your field study already.

John: No, not yet. We ran into a few problems. Some of our specialized equipment hasn't arrived yet. On account of this we may have to put off the field trip until next year.

Sarah: I'm sorry to hear that, but couldn't you leave as soon as the equipment arrives?

John: Well, ordinarily we might, but in view of the fact that the field trip was to be in Antarctica, there's yet another problem.

Sarah: Really? What's that?

John: Well, it's almost winter there now, and since our study will take several months, we'll have to wait at least until next spring. It's just too cold to do much outdoor study there in the winter.

Sarah: Well, it's too bad about having to cancel your field trip, but since you're still in town, why don't you come over for a visit tonight?

John: I was hoping you'd say that! I'd love to.

Listen In

Listen to the lecture again. Notice how these words make it easy for you to hear the shift from an idea to the reason for it. To reinforce this skill and to make certain you will be able to apply it, use one of the following expressions to complete each of the sentences.

because	owing to
because of	in view of that fact
since	for this reason
on account of	

1. The polar regions are unique among the regions of the earth

   _____

   even though they are cold and desolate, they enormously influence the world's climate.

2. _____

   the polar regions are icy deserts, only hardy forms of life can survive there.

3. _____ it

   is quite odd that the penguin chose this land as home.

4. The penguins can fast for some time

   _____ they

   have fed constantly up to that point.

5. They have the energy to swim the hundreds of miles they

   must travel _____

   their previous feeding.

6. _____ many

   birds converge at the same time, order and tidiness are needed.

7. Mates treat each other graciously, perhaps

   _____ all

   the struggles they have endured before mating.

8. _____

   these struggles, some penguins are injured.

9. _____ the

   penguin's good nature, they often share childcare.

10. The sea leopard successfully attacks penguins.

    _____ the

    group is smaller when it returns to the mating ground.

Speak Out

Exercise 1   In order to provide the public with the opportunity to observe ecosystems in urban areas, zoos and wild animal parks are built. To practice the words you studied in the previous exercise, do one of the following activities.

1. If you have been to a zoo or wild animal park, describe it to your class. Use the words for stating reasons from "Skill B" and answer these questions:

   a. Why do you think the zoo or park was built?
   b. Why did you go there?

Hosts and guests at a wild animal park in Texas.

    c. Why do most people go there?
    d. Are the animals well cared for?
    e. Do you think the animals are content or do you think they suffer because they are not in the wild? Why?

2. If you have not been to a zoo or animal park, are you in favor of or against zoos or wild animal parks? Tell why, using at least three of the expressions for stating reasons from "Skill B."

Exercise 2 Now that you've heard the lecture on penguins, consider again your imaginary field study of penguins. Discuss why you would or would not like to take such a trip, using the expressions suggested in "Skill B." What facts about penguins would you want to learn before the trip? What specific behaviors would you want to watch for and why?

CHAPTER 12
LIVING TOGETHER ON A SMALL PLANET

Getting along together in this small space we call Earth is probably life's most important task. Sometimes, however, this is quite difficult for us. To help us, our relatives, teachers, and friends give us moral advice, or thoughts to live by. One example is the Golden Rule: "Do unto others as you would have them do unto you." That is, you should treat others as you would like them to treat you. These thoughts to live by stick in our minds and guide our actions.

Sometimes, when people tell us how to live, we resist even if we know the advice is good. However, when the advice is stated in such a way that it makes us laugh at ourselves, we are more likely to take the advice and more willing to make changes in our behavior. In the lecture in this chapter, you will hear how some famous Americans have looked critically at America and helped us to laugh at ourselves, to put our failings or faults in better perspective.

Lecture: Laughing at Ourselves

Skill A: Summarizing

Skill B: Telling a Joke

PART ONE

DISCUSSION

In small groups, discuss the following.

1. Most cultures have sayings or folk wisdom that children learn as a part of growing up. "Don't bite the hand that feeds you" and "Look before you leap" are examples from English. Think of sayings or proverbs in your native language. Translate them into English and share them with the group. Are any of the sayings humorous? Do you react differently to the humorous sayings than to the more serious ones? Why or why not?

2. Think of particular advice that your mother, father, grandparents, or perhaps a wise uncle or aunt has given to you. Share this advice with your group. Is any of this advice humorous? If so, why do you think so—that is, what makes it humorous?

3. Discuss your impressions of the humor you've experienced from various cultures (during this class discussion and at other times). For example, what makes people of various cultures laugh? Is humor mostly visual or mostly verbal? Do people laugh mainly

at real events or stories they tell? What types of events or stories?

4. Is humor always appropriate? For example, are funny teachers more effective at getting students to learn? Why or why not?

VOCABULARY

Of course by now you know that English words may have multiple meanings. Look over the following list of words from the lecture to see how they will be used in the lecture in this chapter.

ain't	*nonstandard English contraction of* am not, is not, *or* are not
chastity	*restraint, modesty, and purity*
colloquial	*characteristic of informal rather than formal English*
conscience	*feeling of moral responsibility*
counsel	*guidance from a knowledgeable person*
folly	*foolishness*
hain't	*nonstandard English contraction of* has *or* have not
moralist	*a person who comments on what is right and wrong*
pretension	*an air of inviting admiration or an act intended to make one seem better than one really is (in terms of class or morals)*
vanity	*excessive pride, egotism*

Now apply these definitions by choosing the sentence in which the italicized word is used correctly. The first one is done for you.

1. folly

    a. _____ A student's *folly* will probably help him or her to make friends.

    b. _____ Generally, people see the *folly* right after summer when the leaves turn red and gold.

    c. __X__ A friend may sometimes help us see the *folly* of our ways.

2. chastity

    a. _____ The little girl in the white dress, ribbons in her hair, her hands folded in her lap and her eyes cast down, is the perfect picture of *chastity*.

    b. _____ He left his *chastity* on the counter at the bank.

    c. _____ Many people donate money to a favorite *chastity* at Christmas time.

3. counsel

a. _____ Please *counsel* the hotel reservations for next weekend.

b. _____ Many people seek *counsel* when they have to make important decisions.

c. _____ If you want to make a lot of friends, be sure to give *counsel* as soon as you can, before anyone asks for it.

4. moralist

a. _____ The advice of a *moralist* can be helpful and at the same time quite annoying.

b. _____ A *moralist* is someone who always takes a second serving of food at dinner.

c. _____ The ecological study of the moors in England was done by a qualified *moralist*.

5. colloquial

a. _____ His *colloquial* dress made him stand out from the rest of the group.

b. _____ His manner of speaking was very *colloquial,* but since this was a very informal situation it was quite all right.

c. _____ He was known to everyone in town as a *colloquial* character.

6. pretension

a. _____ He went from city to city searching for the best *pretension.*

b. _____ She made elaborate *pretensions* to being generous, but when her friends or relatives asked her for money, she always refused.

c. _____ Your friends will appreciate it if you pay *pretension* when they are speaking to you.

7. conscience

a. _____ The idea was very *conscience,* not at all abstract.

b. _____ His *conscience* was aching, so his wife gave him an aspirin.

c. _____ His *conscience* told him to turn in the $500 he picked up in front of the cafeteria to the lost and found department.

8. vanity

a. _____ *Vanity* is something parents try to develop in their children.

b. _____ The *vanity* in his neck stuck out whenever he got angry.

c. _____ His *vanity* was unbelievable! He looked at himself in every window as he walked down the street.

PART TWO

SKILL A: SUMMARIZING

Consider these situations: You have just read an excellent book and want to tell a friend about it. You have seen a thrilling movie and want to persuade your instructor to go see it. You have heard a fantastic lecture, and you want to share your newfound knowledge with a roommate.

How can you best convey this type of information? You could tell everything you remember about the book, movie, or lecture, but you will probably just want to select the major points or highlights and tell these to your listener. This, of course, is called summarizing. Throughout this book, you have been developing skills to help you summarize. For example, you have learned to listen for the main idea and key terms and to outline and paraphrase what you've heard.

To create a good summary—one that is both accurate and concise—you need to follow two steps. First, gather information by reading, taking notes, or listening carefully for the main points or highlights. Second, organize your thoughts carefully so that your summary is as brief as possible but still accurate and complete. Your audience will help you decide how thorough you need to be. If you are presenting your summary to an instructor, perhaps for an examination, it will need to be extremely complete as well as accurate. You will need to keep in mind any clues your instructor might have given you during the lecture to indicate what he or she considers especially important. If you are summarizing a movie for a friend, you can be less thorough. You might describe one scene in detail and skip several important ones, for example. Or you might refrain from giving away a surprise ending.

Terms such as the following are frequently used to signal important points to remember:

in sum
in summary
to sum up
to summarize

Here are two handy hints to remember about summarizing:

1. Part of the task of summarizing is knowing what to include and what to leave out. There is no need to summarize jokes, interruptions, or other digressions in a lecture, for instance.

2. Generally, you should not try to summarize a short quotation. If the quotation is carefully worded and states a main point, your summary may end up being longer than the original quotation.

Listen In

Listen to the lecture "Laughing at Ourselves" once to get the main ideas.

Then listen to the lecture again. This time, take notes. When you have finished listening and taking notes, write a short summary about the following people, including information about their lifestyles and humorous sayings. Share and discuss your responses with your classmates.

1. Benjamin Franklin

_____

_____

_____

_____

_____

_____

_____

_____

_____

_____

_____

2. Abraham Lincoln

_____

_____

_____

_____

_____

_____

_____

_____

_____

_____

_____

_____

_____

_____

3. Mark Twain

_____

_____

_____

_____

_____

_____

_____

_____

_____

_____

_____

_____

Speak Out

Exercise 1   When completed, the following sayings should sum up a way of looking at life. In small groups, toss out some phrases to complete these sayings. Select the group's two favorites to share with the rest of the class. An example for the first item is provided.

1. Two people can keep a secret if . . .

> **Example:**   one lives on a houseboat in Antarctica, the other lives in Siberia, and neither one has electricity or mail service

2. People will forgive others anything except . . .

3. If you want something done well . . .

4. There are three kinds of teachers . . .

5. There are only three things necessary to keep your wife happy . . .

6. There are only three things necessary to keep your husband happy . . .

7. When angry, count to four; when very angry . . .

8. Sometimes I feel as out of place as . . .

9. Every person with an idea also has . . .

Exercise 2   Read the following quotations. In groups of two to four, devise brief miniplays that illustrate the main ideas of the quotations. Don't tell the rest of the class which quotation you are acting out. Allow the class to guess which quotation best summarizes your skit.

1. "Everyone is ignorant—only on different subjects."—Will Rogers

2. "Everything is funny as long as it's happening to someone else."—Will Rogers

3. "Do not do unto others as you . . . [want them to] do unto you. Their tastes may not be the same."—G. B. Shaw

4. "A loving person lives in a loving world. A hostile person lives in a hostile world: Everyone you meet is your mirror."—Ken Keyes, Jr.

5. "I believe I found the missing link between animal and civilized man. It is us."—Konrad Lorenz

6. "The worst sin towards our fellow creatures is not to hate them, but to be indifferent to them; that's the essence of inhumanity."—G. B. Shaw

7. "I've known a lot of troubles in my time—and most of them never happened."—Mark Twain

8. "You can look at a cup as being either half empty or half full."—proverb

9. "A bore is a man who, when you ask him how he is, tells you."—Burt Leston Taylor

10. "Better to be quarreling than lonesome."—Irish proverb

SKILL B: TELLING A JOKE

Humor is valued in English-speaking countries, and it is common to hear your doctor, dentist, teacher, friends, or acquaintances tell jokes. Sharing laughter is a good way to put other people at ease; it helps create harmony on this small yet complicated planet of ours.

People usually clearly indicate when they are about to tell a joke. Lecturers often do this so that listeners can just relax and listen and not worry about taking notes. The following phrases are commonly used to introduce a joke and are appropriate in any situation in which the joke is appropriate.

Did you hear the one about . . . ?
Have you heard the one about . . . ?
I like the one about . . .
I love to tell the one about . . .
Let me tell you the one about . . .

Once there was . . .
Speaking about (cars, children, money, etc.), have you heard . . . ?
That reminds me of the one about . . .

Listen to Larry Loon, a visiting "stand-up" comedian, introducing his jokes.

Hello folks! Thanks for inviting me to your class. I love visiting classrooms. Sometimes teachers and students have the funniest conversations. Did you hear the one about the teacher who was lecturing about how machines help people? She asked one student, "John, can you name a great time-saver?" And John replied, "Love at first sight."

Ah, yes! I'm really glad to be visiting here. I've never been to this town and I love being a tourist, except that it's so hard to find your way around in a new town sometimes. Let me tell you the one about the tourist who asked the policeman, "Officer, what's the fastest way to the hospital?" The officer replied, "Close your eyes, cross this street, and you'll be there in fifteen minutes."

And that reminds me of the one about the visitor from out of town who asked a friend's little girl, "Anna, when you get as big as your mother, what will you do?" Anna answered quite seriously, "Diet."

Anna sounds quite sure of herself. Let's hope she doesn't grow up to be so sure of herself that she becomes really bossy. That would be too bad. I love the one about the woman who was so bossy that her husband insisted she see a psychiatrist. The wife consented, and the couple went to a doctor. The husband waited outside. When his wife emerged after the hour-long session, he asked, "Did you make any progress?" "Not much," she replied. "It took me fifty minutes to convince that man that his couch would look better against the wall on the other side of the room."

Speaking of women, two women were having lunch in a French restaurant. "You speak Romance languages," said the first. "Get the waiter for us." The second woman raised her hand and said, "Oh, darling . . ."

Well, that's it, folks. It's been swell! And thanks so much!

Listen In

Listen to the lecture again. Because the lecturer uses quotations from famous people and not jokes, he does not indicate when the humor is coming with comments such as "Let me tell you the one about." However, he does pause and change the rhythm or pace of his speaking. When you listen to the lecture, try to be aware of pauses and changes in rhythm and pace. Use these cues to help you pay close attention to the humor, the quotations. Write down key words in the quotations so that you can repeat them and possibly use them in your conversations later. To help you, the first five words are given. Use short forms and abbreviations where possible.

Quotations

Franklin

1. Early to bed, early to . . .

   _____

2. Keep your eyes wide open . . .

   _____

3. Three may keep a secret . . .

   _____

4. If you want a thing . . .

   _____

5. There never was a good . . .

   _____

Crockett

6. Make sure you're right, then . . .

   _____

Lincoln

7. You can fool all of . . .

   _____

8. The Lord prefers common-looking people . . .

   _____

Twain

9. Hain't we got all the . . .

   _____

10. There are three kinds of . . .

11. The reports of my death . . .

Speak Out

Exercise 1   Do you know someone who is almost always funny? Most of us do. And most of us enjoy being around people like this, because they encourage us to laugh at the world and at ourselves. In groups, answer the following questions.

1. Who is your favorite comedian?
2. What is his or her style like? What is so funny about this person?
3. How can a joke be delivered effectively? Ineffectively?

Exercise 2   The following activities may be done separately or combined by using the jokes for Activity 1 in Activity 2.

1. Come to class prepared to tell two jokes that you think are *really* funny and share them with your classmates.
2. Divide into groups of four or five. Each group should be given a topic to discuss. Choose from the following if you wish: work, school, sports, dating, marriage, children, politics, television. Discuss the topic for ten or twenty minutes. As often as possible, interject a joke or a saying into the conversation. Keep score. The group with the most jokes or sayings wins and then must tell its jokes and sayings to the class.

Charlie Chaplin, a comic actor with universal appeal.

149

Answers to Brain Teasers, page 14

1. Zero, because 0 times *anything* is 0.

2. The answer will be 111,111,111, no matter which digit is used.

3. Mary is only five years old and cannot reach the button for the twelfth floor.

4. None. Pigs can't talk.

5. The letter *m*.

6. Just divide the answer by 4 and you will have the number your partner started with.

7. a. The farmer first takes the sheep across the river and leaves it there.
   b. He then returns and takes the lion across the river.
   c. He leaves the lion on the other side and takes the sheep back to the first side.
   d. Then he takes the hay over to the other side and leaves the hay there with the lion.
   e. Finally, he returns for the sheep and the job is done.

8. One. To get the answer, you must draw a family tree. In this one, the governor is A, his wife is a, and his guest is D.

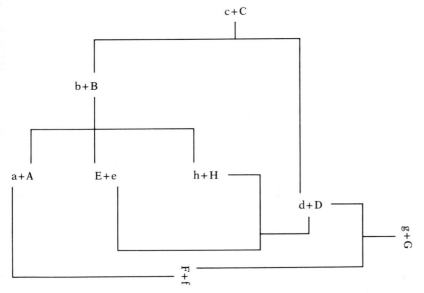

A= the governor of Goleta
a= the governor's wife
B= the governor's father
b= the governor's mother
C= the governor's grandfather
c= the governor's grandmother
D= the governor's father's brother-in-law
d= the governor's father's sister
E= the governor's brother
e= the governor's sister-in-law
F= the governor's father-in-law
f= the governor's mother-in-law
G= the governor's father-in-law's father
g= the governor's father-in-law's mother

Crossword Solution, page 69

		1				2	
1 B	R	E	E	D		L	
3		N	**2** B	O	R	R	O	W
P		V				A	
3 I	R	R	I	G	A	T	I	O	N
O		R					
P		O					
O		N		**4**		
S		M		I		
A		E	**4**	S	N	A	I	L	S
L		N		V		
S		T		E		
5		W	A	S	T	E
		L		S		
		6	S	T	O	C	K

151